HF
5382.6
G65
1996

P9-DMG-439

HF
5382.6
.G65
*1996

Goldman, Katherine Wyse.
    If you can raise kids,
you can get a good job

DATE DUE

SEP 3 0			
OCT 9			
JAN 0 5			

LIBRARY/LRC
OUACHITA TECHNICAL COLLEGE
P.O. BOX 816
MALVERN, ARKANSAS 72104

If You Can
Raise Kids,
You Can Get
a Good Job

Also by Katherine Wyse Goldman

My Mother Worked and I Turned Out Okay

If You Can Raise Kids, You Can Get a Good Job

Katherine Wyse Goldman

HarperCollins*Publishers*

OUACHITA TECHNICAL COLLEGE

Copyright © 1996 by Garret Press, Inc. All rights reserved. Printed in
the United States of America. No part of this book may be used or
reproduced in any manner whatsoever without written permission
except in the case of brief quotations embodied in critical articles and
reviews. For information address HarperCollins Publishers, Inc.,
10 East 53rd Street, New York, NY 10022.

HarperCollins books may be purchased for educational, business, or sales
promotional use. For information please write: Special Markets
Department, HarperCollins Publishers, Inc., 10 East 53rd Street,
New York, NY 10022.

FIRST EDITION

Designed by Nancy Singer

———————————

Library of Congress Cataloging-in-Publication Data
Goldman, Katherine Wyse.
If you can raise kids, you can get a good job / Katherine Wyse Goldman.
— 1st ed.
p.   cm.
ISBN 0-06-017338-6
1. Vocational guidance for women. 2. Mothers—Employment. 3. Job
hunting. I. Title.
HF5382.6.G65   1996
650.14'085'2—dc20   95-40182

———————————

96 97 98 99 00 ❖/HC 10 9 8 7 6 5 4 3 2 1

HF
5382.6
.C665
1996

For Robeka and Denise

Acknowledgments

You can't write a book like this without the honesty, warmth, and hard work of many people.

First, I am grateful to the wonderful women who shared their stories with me. They never thought that what they had to say would be interesting, but as they unfolded their lives, they all realized how much their experiences could mean to women who were just beginning to make these kinds of decisions.

Some of these women were happy to let you know who they are. Others wanted to maintain their privacy, and I have respected that. I thank them all.

I am grateful once again to Diane Reverand, my inspiring and loyal editor, who knew that women wanted to hear from other women. I also thank Meaghan Dowling, who practices the fine art of editing with style.

I thank Jane Dystel, my agent, who works hard and never quits.

I thank good friends and believers who helped me get it done: Sharyn Rosenblum, Rebecca Schulman, Liz Campion, and Cindy Greenfield.

I thank my mother, Lois Wyse, because she too believes and passed along the writing genes in the first place.

And I thank my precious family: Henry, for his wisdom, common sense, and supportive prodding; Max and Molly for their sweetness, love, and ability to get their own snacks when I was on the phone.

Repeat after me: There are fourteen reasons every returning mother can get a good job.

Going to work.

It doesn't look as easy, as instinctive, as forgiving as raising children. But we all know in our heart of hearts that motherhood is rather demanding. Every day another fireball could be tossed your way. If I say this, will my child slam the door? If I do that, will my child run away this week? You're constantly negotiating for the little dears—with teachers who don't understand them, with grandparents who want to spoil them rotten, and with other parents who let their kids jump naked out of low-flying aircraft.

After that, what's so scary about finding a job?

Defining yourself? Calling complete strangers on the phone? Convincing yourself you can do something? Assuming your children can pack their lunches and put a load into the washer without supervision?

Look at the other side. Going to work is filled with assurances, the promise of a bright future, your very own money in your pocket. And there are fourteen reasons you're going to get there.

Every mother in this book taught me that.

So here they are. Memorize them. And repeat them to yourself before, during, and after every job interview.

1.   There's no right time to get married, have children, or go back to work.
2.   Of course there's something you can do.
3.   Returning to school as a mother-student is a lot more fun than going as the mother of students.
4.   You can convince anybody that "Mother" on your resume means contractor, comptroller, purchasing agent, personnel manager, judge, corrections officer, and tenured professor.
5.   No matter how many millions you've volunteered to raise for others, it makes a difference when it's going into your own checking account.
6.   Now that you've nurtured the dreams of everybody else, it's their turn to encourage yours.
7.   There are certain things that happen in the working world that will come as naturally to you as carrying enough Kleenex, checking to see if the baby is breathing, and whirling around every time you hear a child say "Mom."

8.   Nine to five in a glass office building is not everybody's idea of happiness.

9.   You'll be welcomed eagerly to the World of Guilty Working Mothers.

10. It won't be long before words like *nanoseconds, quality initiatives, networking, databases,* and *macroeconomics* are tripping off your tongue.

11. Your career path can look as clear as a Rorschach inkblot.

12. From the other side of the desk, you'll be putting other moms back to work.

13. There will come a day when the judge's robe, surgeon's mask, Armani suit, corner office, and key to the executive washroom are all within your grasp.

14. You can be proud of your children's accomplishments and your own at the same time.

A mother first.

At first, I think I just wanted to be pregnant. You don't have to worry about holding in your stomach, you're not even allowed to exercise vigorously, and you're forced to get a whole new wardrobe.

I loved going to work and having people offer me their seats on the bus and I eagerly accepted everyone's compliments about my wonderful glow.

I knew there was a baby coming at some point. I saw enough of them being pushed around in strollers and carried in Snuglis, but I didn't understand what was really going to happen—that the focus of my life was about to change. I had never been much of a baby-sitter when I was in high school, so I didn't know about babies. Fortunately, my mother had had some experience and took me on a shopping expedition for tiny undershirts, sheets, crib pads and liners and bumpers so at least I'd be prepared. But when my husband and I shopped for furniture, we were bewildered. A huge assortment of cribs and changing tables and carseats? How were we to know what to buy when we didn't even know the personality of the user?

And just about every week the man who ran the advertising

agency where I worked would call me in and ask me about my plans for the future. I assumed I was going back to work right away. I couldn't even *begin* to comprehend how women could stay home with children. I had this great career—a real life. Besides, my mother had always worked, and I saw most of the women of my generation staying in their jobs. I didn't think being home with children was any kind of life at all.

Then our son was born, and my view of things changed—I suddenly discovered it's fun to be a mother.

It was kootchy-kootchy-koo, that toothless grin, that soft skin, those teeny toes, that spot under the chin that begs to be kissed. That unparalleled love without question. That first turn in the crib, the little fingers poking out from under the bumper pads, the strong little back, the first creep, the first crawl, the first monster step. You've got to be there.

And I really had to be there because my official maternity leave, counting extra sick days and vacation days and disability time (disability?) was just five weeks. I cradled my newborn in my arms and said to my boss, "How can I leave him? I'm not coming back to work."

I couldn't believe it was me talking.

But he was so cute, so endearing, so soft. On the other hand, he slept so much, and he couldn't carry on a conversation. It took forever to get out of the house, and when I finally emerged, I always had to carry a big bag of baby stuff. I felt like an invalid receiving reports from everyone else about what was going on in the world. I called a friend who had left her big career to take care of her three children and asked, "What do you do all day?" She recited a litany of household and childhood activities from play groups to movement classes to multiple loads of laundry and making living room curtains that had me feeling like I was going to be washed down a drain. I was crazy about my son, but I could never make anybody happy if my only thoughts centered on people who had never even read a book. Things had to change.

So after four months, when I had learned how to get dressed before one in the afternoon and had had enough baby-sitters not to think every one probably had a police record, I gingerly went out into the world to work. But not full-time. I chose freelance so that I could be around for my son. I wanted the freedom to choose when to work so I could go on field trips, get to the school plays, and take my son to museums during the week.

In my life as a mother of two, I've seen many women wrestling every single day with the same issues. Because while the children are little, it's wonderful to be with them. There's nothing like that experience. And, true, it's over before you know it.

In almost a split second, the children are independent and would rather live like Pippi Longstocking. They can get their own cereal in the morning, pour milk without spilling, remember to take their vitamins, fold their clothes, order a pizza, make their own play dates, tie their own soccer shoes, plug in plugs, play Monopoly (the grown-up one), figure out the VCR, and even read to themselves at night, thank you.

Suddenly, they don't need you there every single second.

And you, suddenly, need something other than them to define your life.

Because if you've stayed home with your children to be there for the milestones, your life has been defined as the mother of a newborn, a toddler, a preschooler.

You're the carpooler, the neighbor to call in an emergency, the volunteer for everything.

And you think: What happened to that college education? Where did that drive and ambition to be a movie star, a nurse, a doctor, a teacher, an executive, a firefighter disappear to? What's that little spark in your heart when you think about earning your own money, having your own schedule and a set of responsibilities that don't include anyone whose diaper you have ever changed?

You're about to change your life.

You're a Returning Mother. A woman who has known the joys of being with her children and now wants to return to the workforce or join it for the first time.

You might not have the faintest idea what you're going to do. Or you might be applying to vet school because you've wanted to do it since you were seven. You might turn your ten years of volunteer work into a business you never dreamed of running. You and the mother of your daughter's best friend could decide to be caterers together. Do these seem like possibilities?

Anything's possible. Because the work we do every day as mothers is practically impossible. We shape the emotional, physical, and intellectual lives of human beings, transform babies who are completely dependent upon us into adults who are completely independent from us. We plan menus, shop, cook, balance the budget, mediate squabbles, master pediatric medicine, negotiate with plumbers, electricians, and carpenters, raise money, and plan fund-raising events. Nobody's ever going to put all that in your job description. But nobody will put finding sock mates and picking up prescriptions from the all-night drugstore in your job description, either.

I've met women at all stages of working and parenting. I know what it's like to feel guilty because you're not out there working. I know what it's like to have a vision of yourself sitting in a big office but having no idea how to find the elevator that will take you there. And I know what it's like to have to defend your decision to stay home with your children—while you do the most important job of all.

I wrote a book, *My Mother Worked and I Turned Out Okay*, in which adults spoke of the many benefits they derived from having had a working mother. While I traveled around the country after the book was published, talking to working mothers, many moms who were still at home with their children told me they wanted to go back to work someday but were unsure how to do it. Many had worked but didn't want to go back into the professions they had left. Some feared they would be out of touch with the latest trends or methods; others worried about competing with eager twenty-two-year-olds. Some wished that they could invent the Pet Rock or that the perfect job would just be thrown into their laps. Many wanted a flexible schedule, as they weren't ready yet to leave their children until six-thirty at night. They wondered whether it was worth it to disrupt their family life, asked what happens if you hate your job, and worried how their teenagers would fare in the new, temptation-filled world of after school. They wondered whether any employer in the world would think they still had a brain after raising children.

I listened to their stories, to their confusion, and then went out to find women who had done it. Women who had been home to their satisfaction, then built new lives for themselves. I went out to look for Returning Mothers.

I found them everywhere. And I discovered that many career women we see around us took time off from their careers to raise their children before returning to work. Madeleine Albright, the

American ambassador to the United Nations, didn't even start working until her three children were in school. Supreme Court Justice Sandra Day O'Connor left the law for years to raise her sons.

I also found women who bumped along like the rest of us. Women who made all kinds of compromises and structured crazy schedules so they could go to work as nurses, clerks, stockbrokers, lawyers, teachers, entrepreneurs, politicians, chefs, merchants, environmental activists, and bankers.

Most now have grown children, and many still raise youngsters and work with flexible schedules they have devised with their employers. Many returning mothers found support groups that helped them while they were at home, then again when they were ready to reenter the workforce. These mothers have all kinds of ideas for keeping up while you're at home and for being successful when you go back to work.

They didn't do it without difficulty. But they did it. They are happy with the choices they made and the way their lives have turned out. Their stories are inspirational, though they'd never describe them that way.

They're moms, after all, like you. And they did exactly what you want to do. Their words and their experiences should give you the courage to pursue your new life. Once they felt as you do: that they were great mothers who loved and adored their children, but that if they didn't get out and work, faltering self-esteem or monstrous college costs would get them first. And they, too, worried that an employer would look at them and say, "What the hell have you been doing for the last five years?"

Now they say, "If you can raise kids, you can get a good job."

There's no right time to get married, have a baby, or go back to work.

Mothers are so great at telling everybody when they're supposed to do everything.

They know precisely how long it takes each family member to get up and out of the house in the morning. They know exactly how many days in advance to begin a term paper. They know how long it takes to fill out college applications.

They want everybody to plan, plan, plan. Organize, organize, organize.

Yet the watchword of every mother alive is *carpe diem*, or seize the day—within reason, of course.

All mothers know that we don't walk around with Mickey Mouse alarm clocks in our heads that clang relentlessly to signal one stage of life has passed and another is to begin on schedule. Our lives blur and blend. We know it's okay if one of our children is reading beautifully at age four and the next must be bribed to read at age six. You might have invested a small fortune in a small violin, only to have your child come home one day wanting to play the tuba because nobody else does. We're able to pick up and move across the country when opportunity knocks even if we've just redone the kitchen.

Mothers know that none of the big important stuff happens on schedule anyway. And that's one reason many mothers choose to stay home with their children. Because as much as you want your baby to do everything on schedule, there's no telling when he's going to smile or say "Mama" or receive his first gash requiring stitches. You never know the exact moment your child will need a special hug, a secure hand to hold, a quiet talk, or a cozy cuddle on your lap.

Besides, the best stories in your life are those about the unexpected, about how you met your husband, about how your baby arrived in a taxicab. Sure, you're sort of ready for things to happen. That's how you know you should pay attention. The new experiences make your life much more interesting.

There's absolutely no way you can know when to schedule those big life changes. That night I took my seat at the ballet, I never knew I would be meeting my future husband at intermission or that I would be picking up and moving to Philadelphia just when my career was progressing.

Then we had our children twenty months apart. You know how many opinions there are on that subject? I was validated when finally I found a magazine article detailing the benefits of having children close together. But all I had to do was look at my own two children becoming terrific buddies to know we hadn't committed the cardinal sin of parenting. And there are just as many women who have children years and years apart who have to listen to the tsk-tskers.

Whoever wrote the rules on when to do everything was wrong.

The time you fall into everything is pretty much right.

There's a whole generation of women out there who were given a nice easy set of rules to follow: Nice girls marry when the right boy comes along, have children one, two, three, and change their curtains twice a year.

Not all these women were completely satisfied with that neat little package.

Dorie fell into the working world quite unexpectedly. She was married a week after her nineteenth birthday, assumed the life of a wife, and got her success through her husband. She had always thought she had to marry someone with good prospects. He did well. It was the good life. But he died when she was in her thirties, and she was left with a six-year-old daughter.

"I could have lived on the money he left me, but I was born to work. My friends thought it was strange that I wanted to do anything, but I wanted the discipline. And I came to the realization that I had to do something with the rest of my life."

She got a lead the way many of us do—through a friend who called and told her about a television station looking for a woman to cohost a show for investors in the stock market and talk to them about culture. She loved the idea, but by the time she got to the station, the position was filled. Unwilling to give up, she convinced the owner that he needed her to serve coffee and trot the guests in and out. He hired her at seventy-five dollars a week.

"It was nirvana," she says. "Then when it was quite obvious that this pretty young hostess they had hired for the show was not up to it, they moved me in quickly. I worked happily for two and a half years, until the ax fell and the entire cast was dumped. But I had found my bliss, and no one was going to do me out of it. I knew that my energy and passion would land me on my feet."

It didn't take long. She heard that a station in town was looking for someone to be a liaison to the community. She convinced the general manager she was the one to hire, then sent him a list every ten days of everything she could do for the station. Twenty-five years later she has an office full of awards and Emmys. Says Dorie, "It's only because I knew I wanted something."

Some women are absolutely positive that they will go back to work, and they know exactly when they'll do it. How *do* they know that? Well, some put a date on it. When the youngest child is six years old seems to be a popular time, when the children have finally gone to school. But figuring out exactly how something will happen can get in your way.

Frances had made up her mind to go back to teaching when her first child turned six. But it didn't turn out to be as smooth a transition as she had hoped. "My husband kept taking sabbaticals, we'd uproot the family, and I had to keep thinking of new things to do when I came back," she says. As a result, she found she was capable of finding various freelance assignments writing elementary-level educational materials with a college friend who also was looking for work.

Patti decided, too, that she'd go back when her youngest was in first grade, but she found she couldn't wait until then. "How do you say no when you're offered the perfect job?" she asks.

She had been a flight attendant, then done marketing for another airline before her children were born. After her three months' maternity leave, her husband was transferred to St. Louis. "It was too hard for me to be in a new place, find a new job, and take care of a new baby, so I quit," she says.

She wasn't sure what she would do, but she knew she wanted to go back to work at some point. She became friendly with a woman whose partner had taken a maternity leave from their business escorting authors who came to town on publicity tours. When the woman's partner moved away, Patti took her place.

"It was just the right kind of career for me," says Patti. "My children were small enough that I wanted the flexibility to be with them. Now it's been ten years, the children are grown and gone, and I still love it. And I'm using my head every single day."

Waiting until your child is six years old might seem ideal, but that option presents its own obstacle to joining the workforce. It's after school, that time in which kids take karate, swimming, gymnastics, violin, or art lessons, when they do homework and crave play dates. I've always found it to be an incredibly difficult period of time. And if your children don't have thousands of activities, they come home at three in the afternoon, which is not exactly the end of the day for the rest of the world. It's a little tough to raise your hand at two-thirty and say to your boss, "Excuse me, I have to leave this important meeting. My children will be home soon, and they're too young to let themselves into the house."

So much for the right time for everyone.

Many mothers these days have lived a whole life before they got married and had children. Because they already have had their career, they're ready to leave and be there while the children grow up.

To a point.

Anna had always taught and was in her second marriage when she had her first child. "I got to do a lot before I had children," she says. "I was more mature, more stable. But when my daughter was born, I just wanted to be home. I had waited so long to have a baby. I was rather disappointed, though, because I wanted her to walk and talk, not just lie there. My husband presumed I would stay home. I told him that eventually I wanted to go back to work.

"Years later, the school where I had taught started to bug me about coming back. I thought, 'I've stayed home, I've made cookies. The children walk in and out, and I'm still here.' So I went to talk to the school administrators. Once I was in, I thought, 'It's calling me.'"

She went home and *told* her husband she was going back. She didn't discuss it.

"What will you do with the children?" he asked.

"'I'll get a baby-sitter,'" I told him. I didn't find a woman to take care of the children until the night before I was going back. She didn't believe I was going to work the next morning. 'If you take the children, I'll never ask you to do anything again,' I told her.

"I've been back teaching for thirty years, and I love it. No two classes or two years are the same. It's an ever-changing job. Every morning I think, 'I'm going to work. I'm going to have a great day.'"

The right time for you may be when your self-esteem demands it.

Bea went to work not only to have a more interesting life but also because she didn't like the way she felt anymore. "When I got married," says Bea, "the idea of a career other than raising a family never occurred to me. As the years went on, it changed. I was raising three children, I had a husband who traveled a lot, and I was left in the background. I didn't think I was taking full advantage of my talents.

"Mostly, I was tired of people asking me what I do. I felt embarrassed. I felt guilty for not going to work. What women do who stay at home is not valued. I wanted to prove I was bright, and I wanted to show the world that someone would pay me to do a job. That's what sent me back to college."

These days, though, women can find a lot of support among the other moms who are at home. Because so many women have already had careers and the accompanying stimulation, financial rewards, and ego gratification, it's not easy to forgo those benefits.

One national support group is called FEMALE, which

stands for Formerly Employed Mothers at the Leading Edge. One of the directors is Linda Rush, who was gainfully employed, took her maternity leave when her child was born, returned to work, and says, "I was not happy, my husband was not happy. I lasted two weeks in my job." She became a mother-at-home but understands that "once women have gotten the self-esteem from the workforce, it's very hard to give it up."

A poll of FEMALE members shows how many of these moms want to become returning mothers. The average age of their members is thirty-three, and the average amount of time they stay home is three years. And 97 percent of them say they're going back to work. When? Four percent say immediately. Nine percent say when the youngest child enters preschool. Forty-nine percent say when the youngest is in kindergarten. Five percent say when the youngest goes to high school. Another 5 percent say when the youngest graduates from high school. And the remaining 28 percent? They don't know. See, you're not alone.

Some women don't think there's any right time for them to go back to work. They never built it into their plans. Jane surely didn't have working in mind as she enjoyed the country-club life without a care in the world. But her husband changed all that when he took off with a younger woman after twenty-five years of marriage. He left Jane with a luxurious lifestyle and no way to pay for it.

Her daughters were pointed toward careers, but Jane didn't even know how to write a check. She needed a full-time job, but what could she do? Her local community college had a course for returning mothers. She enrolled in the four-month course and learned from the professional women who taught her how to balance her checkbook, write a resume, and find a job as a secretary.

"I'm fifty-two now, and I feel better about myself than I ever have in my life," says Jane. "I'm happy I found out what I can do."

"You know, if my husband hadn't left me, I never would have gone back to work. I would have stayed in that dependent situation. I never would have had this feeling I have now. That would have been too bad because there's nothing like it.

"I should have had more confidence in myself, seeing how I did raising my children. They're wonderful. And now I'm thrilled with working—and with my kids."

Of course there's something you can do.

Changing everything that is familiar, putting yourself on the line, trying to transform your motherly talents into marketable skills just isn't the easiest thing you could possibly do.

It's so much easier to find other pressing things to do, like laundry.

How can you think about a job when your working wardrobe consists of faded, rumpled sweatpants and T-shirts and you see those working mothers every morning in their tailored suits, perfect scarves, the right pins, panty hose, and real shoes?

What is your talent? How can you possibly assess your own talent?

Where do you begin?

Who do you ask?

What are the rest of the questions, anyway?

It's daunting. Paralyzing.

Don't worry. Mothers before you have figured it out.

Hazel O'Leary, Bill Clinton's Secretary of Energy, was a young mother living in New Jersey, pushing her cart through the supermarket with her two-year-old when she realized it was almost two o'clock, time for her favorite soap opera, *Young Dr. Malone*. She abandoned her cart of groceries in the store and speeded home. When she got there she said to herself, "Good Lord, there's got to be more to life than this."

She called Rutgers University Law School, presented her three-year-old law-school tests and undergraduate records, and was told she could enroll the following month. That action helped her become general counsel for the U.S. Community Services Administration, an assistant prosecutor, an assistant attorney general, and a partner in a national accounting firm before she went into national politics.

Women have to understand they're capable of this kind of action. Alexis is a judge today, but she was home with her children for many years before she pushed herself into the working world.

"People don't move forward unless they move themselves forward," she says. "In the movies a talent scout sees a pretty girl at a drugstore counter and her career is made, but that's not how it happens. Girls learn when they're young that if they're good in school, and they're good people, they'll be rewarded. Someone will recognize them. Too many women are used to being rewarded for having their hands clasped on the desk. But you have to go after what you want."

How do you know what you want?

First of all, figure out what you *like* to do.

It could be very simple. Jean Van Leeuwen is a children's book author by default. When her two children were three and four years old, Jean started writing down the funny things they said and did. Soon she realized that the wonderful antics of her children could be turned into picture books for other children. She created the characters of Oliver and Amanda Pig. She's continued to write over the years and has produced more than twenty books and a wonderful new life for herself.

Elise and her friend Ruth were mothers at home in the Midwest, and they liked to play folk guitar for their children and their friends. One day Ruth got a call from Elise. A local television station had asked whether they would play on a children's program.

"We can't do this!" Ruth said.

"Of course we can," Elise said. "We'll do what we do at home when we play for the kids." That's what they did, and playing on that show led to Ruth's developing a whole new interest in television and a new career as a television producer.

That should teach you always to say "Of course" when somebody asks if you can do something. Never turn down anything that seems remotely interesting. Who knows where it will lead?

It's important to find what you like, what you think is worthwhile. It's not sensible to uproot your existence if the work is something you don't want to spend your time doing. Sherri found this out. Her field was speech pathology, but she stopped working when she was pregnant and she and her husband moved to Missouri, where she would have had to go back for recertification. "It wasn't worth it. I had reached my saturation point anyway. I couldn't give it one hundred percent."

She wanted to stay home and be a mother. Actually, since it had taken her eight years to get pregnant, she thought she should stay home and appreciate the long-awaited baby. "I loved my baby, but I have to admit I was bored," she said.

Then she found something to do. Her husband bought a business, which he ran from home. Sherri thought it would help if she did the books for her husband at night and could be with the baby during the day.

"But I felt very isolated. All I did was go to the grocery store and play group. I still worked for my husband but got a baby-sitter once a week so I could volunteer. It was good to get away from kid stuff. I took workshops to further my education and use my mind."

Finally, they moved the business out of their house, and Sherri kept the hours of her son's preschool. "The business needs me, but it's not what I want at all. It's not a career for me. It's just a little job that keeps my mind occupied.

"I feel I need something else, but I haven't figured it out yet. I always read about women who come up with neat ideas for cottage businesses. I think they're really creative. Some people go their whole lives without finding something. I know I won't do that."

Still, though, she doesn't know how to find the right job.

Well, if you look around you, you'll find the people who can help you answer your questions. There are so many returning mothers these days that many career counselors have refocused their businesses to include and support them.

Vicki Kramer started her firm, Options, in Philadelphia more than twenty years ago, to help women cope with work and family issues. Kramer helped them deal with the conflicts, helped them decide what to do and then to make the decision whether to go back full- or part-time. Women needed counseling. Selling them to corporations in those days was tough. It was daring to hire women.

Her long experience has taught her that returning mothers need to answer two questions first: What do I want to do? and What is marketable about me?

"When I meet these mothers," says Kramer, "I see what has happened to their confidence while they've been home. But think about what you've been doing. There aren't many mothers who stay home to clean the house and watch soap operas anymore, especially the women who had worked before. Now women have done a lot of volunteering, or they've worked part-time in their fields." Your skills and interests are your best paths back to work.

Can your interest really become your career?

Ellie Huggins always loved nature and became a volunteer environmental activist but had no idea it was going to lead her to a career. She discovered that many of the women who were volunteering were bright and talented and wanted to keep their minds active. Together they devised material for classrooms, took kids on field trips, compiled a natural history of the San Francisco Bay Area, and put together an earthquake-education kit.

Then leaders of an organization dedicated to keeping undeveloped land an open space asked her to join them and offered her a part-time paying job. That led to fund-raising and being named director of development. And then an old friend asked her to help write a book on nature.

"Part of my success," Ellie says, "is that I'm not afraid to try anything. I have always remembered what I learned in school: Expand your horizons, and learn to think for yourself."

Your interests could lead you down a new, unexplored career path. The world is changing so fast that the kind of work you become involved in when you return might turn out to be an intriguing new field.

That's what happened to Marsha. She had a history degree from Wellesley but had little time to put it to use before she had children and left the workforce. When she found that her husband was busy in his career and the children were involved in their own lives, she knew she needed something for herself. But what?

"I had worked at the art museum doing conservation," Marsha says, "but I didn't want to spend my life at it. I'd also done some social work at a hospital and had gone into terrible areas. I liked that." So when her youngest went to kindergarten, she enrolled in college for a degree in social work.

While working at the National Council on Alcoholism's

employee assistance program with a woman named Marion, they noticed a significant need in the marketplace. Many clients they saw as social workers were unable to manage their complicated affairs, to deal with lawyers, hospitals, social workers, and bankers. To help the families of the elderly or infirm, the two women went into business as the liaison among all of these people. "We really are like professional mothers," says Marsha. "So many families are scattered, and there is no one to set up nursing care, to arrange for medical assistance.

"When we started out, we couldn't find another company doing this. Now we belong to a professional association. I love what I do and what my job has turned in to."

Sometimes it doesn't seem as though what you like and what you're good at have any practical merit. But once you make your decision, you need to stick with it. Then your interests will mean something to you and the people around you, as Happy Fernandez's story shows.

She was prepared to go to work. She even had a master's in teaching from Harvard, but when Happy and her husband moved to Philadelphia, she was pregnant, and pregnant women were not allowed to teach. So she stayed home with her three sons, and to keep her mind active she volunteered in the community. She had a vibrant ten-year career as a volunteer, emerging as a leader of the parents in a teachers strike. She had shouting matches with the mayor, lobbied city council, was the spokesperson on television. Shortly after that a professor friend asked whether she'd like to teach a course in child advocacy.

"I'm not sure what that is," Happy replied.

"You've been doing it," the friend told her.

She decided to do it, starting with an evening course, then accepting a full-time opening a couple of years later. One evening at a cocktail party she got the inevitable question: "What do you do?"

"I'm teaching."

"What?"

"Child care and child advocacy."

"I got a blank look," says Happy. "It wasn't the same as being a lawyer or a doctor. Child care was considered a child's issue. I felt I wasn't in the mainstream."

It didn't stop her from pursuing her interests. She started a citywide parents' union that advocated for parents' issues, which very few politicians cared about. "When I went to city representatives," she says, "I was treated like a child even though by this time I had three master's degrees."

Then, when a seat became available on the city council, she decided to run for it. Happy was elected. "I learned that if you invest of yourself, it comes back," she reasons. Happy finds that her life has changed measurably and that in addition to accomplishing many goals for her community, she's become more assertive about her needs and more independent, an unexpected benefit of returning to work. Those around her have noticed the difference, too. "Many years ago when I was doing child advocacy," she recalls, "a man said to me, 'You're a tough lady.' I was surprised. I always thought of myself as a nice woman. Now I'd be proud to be called a tough lady. I still want to be a woman. But there's a backbone there."

Returning to school as a mother-student is a lot more fun than going as the mother of students.

Think of the panic that seizes you whenever you hear that the teacher wants to see you. Millions of things run through your mind. Not a single one is positive. Even though you may be the proud parent of the best children who ever lived on the face of the earth, you know they sometimes make mistakes in school. And you're called in as the parole officer.

But let's say you go to the children's school on your own volition. It's probably because you're hawking brownies at the

Valentine's Day bake sale or geraniums at the spring plant sale or novels at the fall book sale.

Or it's Parents' Night.

Or Grandparents' Day.

Or the school play. The soccer game. The swim meet. The class picnic.

What do they do in school anyway?

If you're thinking about going back to work, you might want to find out.

For yourself this time.

Because if you're encouraging your children to go on to college or pursue graduate degrees, doesn't it make sense that further education might help in your new career, too? Once you go back to school as a grown-up, you have a deeper appreciation and higher level of understanding of just how wonderful school can be.

I had the luxury of going back to college a few years ago when my husband was awarded a fellowship at the University of Michigan. One of the greatest benefits of his new position was that I could take any courses the university offered. I looked at the descriptions of graduate courses in English. They seemed so pedantic, focusing on what I considered the minutiae of literature, that I chose a few undergraduate courses. My children were two and three at the time, so I felt as though I hadn't read a book in a decade. I picked courses that demanded tons of reading—all in tiny type. I read Dickens, Eliot, Trollope, James, Conrad, Hardy, Faulkner, and the Bible from beginning to end.

I made notes all over my books. I could hardly wait for class. I asked all kinds of questions. It was a great departure from my degree-producing undergraduate experience. Being back in school gave me the time and space to think about what I wanted to do. I was convinced I wanted to write more than advertising copy.

Many returning mothers are going back to school first. Some come back because they never went to college, or never finished college, or they want to upgrade their skills or learn about a whole new field.

And colleges are adapting to the needs of returning mothers. There's no reason to fear going back to school. Look around and find the program that's looking for you. You deserve the most supportive program you can find, one that recognizes you might not be able to handle a full course load in sequential semesters.

Chatham College in Pittsburgh has one of the best-known programs for returning mothers. The Gateway Program was born in 1974, when women started believing they could do anything. They could not, however, balance the demands of family and college. And no one understood them when they said they needed nurturing or support from other women going through the same things. Except the college president, Edward Eddy. He heard their stories and started Gateway with eleven women.

One of the first students was Barbara Greenberg. She had never finished college, having instead married her husband after sophomore year. When she wanted to go back to college, Chatham was the only college that would accept her ten-year-old credits. She enrolled, graduated, and now she's a director of Gateway.

She has a real understanding of the women who want to enter the program. One night at an orientation, Barbara talked to women about their need for fulfillment. She looked out to see five of them in tears. One's youngest child had just started nurs-

OUACHITA TECHNICAL COLLEGE

ery school, one's youngest was going to kindergarten, one's youngest was going to college, one had lost her husband, and another's husband had left her for his secretary.

The women and their needs were diverse. "The women I started with were all different from me," says Barbara. "By the time you go back to school, you understand that you can learn a lot from a diverse group of people."

Women are taken through the program very carefully, with real attention to their needs. "I've seen women here," Barbara says, "who can't lift their heads because they have no self-esteem. Some never had it because of their upbringing, some lost it through a bad marriage, and some were beaten down in other jobs. We put on a whole program for them because we know this is a total life experience."

The women are given encouragement every step of the way. One forty-eight-year-old woman with two children sobbed through her interview as she described how her husband had left her as she was about to undergo life-threatening surgery. From her entrance essay, the admissions committee recognized she was a wonderful writer with talents she could develop. Eventually, she was elected president of the student association, then went on to do graduate work in anthropology.

"We never accept anyone as a Gateway student who would not succeed academically," says Barbara. "No one needs to fail, and if we see a woman who has been active in volunteer work, we know she can do it." Gateway encourages a woman to start with one course and let her family get settled. And the program gives tips on how a woman can involve her family in the process in a loving, motherly way.

Then, when a returning mother is ready to go to work,

Gateway offers all kinds of support, from career testing to a mentor and internship program to mock job interviewing. Local alums in careers come and meet with students to tell them about what they do.

Along with knowledge and a college degree, many women in the Gateway Program gain a new insight into the work they have done at home. Says Barbara, "Many of the women don't realize all the physical and mental effort it took to raise the children. Work is surprisingly easy. When you're home it's a twenty-four-hour-a-day job. You'll never find something to replace that intensity. You have to move on in a different direction."

Not every college is quite as kind. Don't imagine that you'll find special programs and empathy at every level. At the Wharton School of Business there are executive M.B.A. programs, but they're really geared toward people who are currently involved in careers. Though the average age of the students is thirty-three, they have a sophisticated knowledge of their fields and very specific goals in getting their master's in business.

Coming in as a full-time student is "really tough," says professor Stewart Friedman. "The cult of the student body is such that if you're beyond the traditional age, it's hard to get involved. You have to be immersed in the life here. It's intense. We have team meetings until two in the morning. You have to be prepared to work strenuously. It's shocking even for young bucks who have been on Wall Street."

He does, however, recognize the importance of women in the workforce. "As more and more women become part of the labor pool, the best and the brightest are often checking out at thirty-five. The organization tracks are too rigid and don't allow people to commit to other roles than work. It's a cynical way in which our society underinvests in its future.

"I would love to have some of those women come back full-time to business school," says Friedman. "I would advocate their admission. We need more diversity in terms of age range and family status. I had this epiphany myself when I became a parent. I had had no preparation for or experience with wanting to nurture. Then I saw how difficult it was for my wife and me to balance our families and careers. Business schools have a responsibility to teach students how to connect all this with what organizations do to this balancing act."

When you go back to finish your undergraduate degree, you might like it so much and have so much you want to do that you'll find yourself applying to graduate school. It might be hard to believe now, and it was for Dena, too, who never pictured herself in the workforce to begin with.

"I was a room mother, a docent at the art museum, a fundraiser for everything," she says. "One day someone called and asked whether I would raise funds for a junior symphony. I looked at my book and saw I didn't have a free day for six weeks. It was ridiculous. I wanted some time for myself. So I extricated myself from volunteer things for a year and got good at golf and tennis, but it bored the hell out of me."

Her husband, meanwhile, had a very interesting life and invited fascinating, well-known people to their home for dinner.

But it was a threat to Dena. "I was always a passive person at these parties. I couldn't talk about anything. I lived on the periphery of my own life." She knew it was time to go back to college, so she took some classes at a junior college and loved it.

She was eager to go back full-time even though she and her husband had four kids to send to college. Her husband was unequivocal and encouraged her to enroll in a big university, where she studied foreign policy while Nixon was opening China.

"I felt great about myself. For the first time in years I felt as though men were interested in what I had to say," she says. "I had always found that a nonworking woman can participate in a conversation with men, but after she talks, they go on as if she never said anything."

When she was ready to graduate, and unsure about what to do next, her husband encouraged her to go on to law school because he thought that her problem-solving skills would serve her well in the law. Believing she could make it through law school, she took the LSAT's and went on to a law school that encouraged many returning mothers.

When it came time to think about what to do with the law degree, Dena played it low-key. Her husband had the big, successful, high-profile career. She didn't think it was for her. "I allowed myself to be entirely flexible about a job so if it didn't work out, I wouldn't be so wrapped up emotionally. I was also worried that a big firm was too much commitment, that I would fail and do something irreparable to my husband, my family, and myself." But when a friend of her husband's offered an internship, then an associate's position at a big firm, she took it. It turned out to be a mistake.

"It wasn't a life. It was a sweatshop," she recalls. The firm thought lawyers were sloughing off if they didn't bill two thousand hours a year. After a couple of years, when her husband said he needed vacations and she saw her children only once during their four-day college vacations, she changed firms. This time, though, she did it the way she wanted to.

At the new firm she didn't worry about making partner. She was gutsy. She told the partners up front that she had to have vacations, that she had to travel with her husband to certain meetings. And, yes, she did make partner there.

"I never could have done all this while my children were little," Dena says. "I wanted to be the primary nurturer. Unless you're willing to give that up, you can't be a star in your career. There is power in running the house. For me the career power came at the right time—later."

~~~~~

That later-in-life power can turn out to be formidable.

Louise was a college graduate and home with her husband and four children for eleven years before she knew what she needed. "I thought I could try working in child development, and I tried going back for graduate courses, but it was a very poor fit for me. My own children were enough."

One night she was at a party chatting with a friend and complaining about the path she had chosen. Her friend wondered what Louise would have done had she been a man. "I didn't have an answer, and the question haunted me," she says. She thought about what had happened to the men with whom she was friendly in college and realized that many of them were lawyers. To her it seemed like a crazy idea for a mother of four children between two and eight to go back to law school, but she found a law school that was gracious, encouraging, and would let her go part-time.

"I didn't know what I was getting into, but when I read my first case, I knew I was right. To this day, I retain my enthusiasm and excitement," says Louise from her comfortable chambers where she works on cases these days as an appellate judge.

"I think that if young mothers don't have to go to work, they shouldn't. I'm not sure the children miss anything if the mother is working, but I know the mother does. You're so tired it's hard to enjoy the family.

"But once you're ready to go to work, if you want to have a grand adventure in life, take the next bus that comes along."

Not everyone's plan is quite as grand. If you haven't been in college for some time, start out taking one course. But the way that one little course can change your life can be spectacular. Nancy Byrd found that one college course opened a whole new world she never would have discovered on her own.

Nancy's husband left her when she was eight-and-a-half months pregnant with her third child. She'd been a housewife near Fresno ever since she'd married him ten years before. Now she had to get out of the house and into a job to support her family.

Knowing she had to get some kind of training, she enrolled in an introductory computer course because she thought that in any job she'd have to be able to use one. Her instructor was a woman who had a software business, and they became friendly. She made computers interesting to Nancy, so much so that computers themselves became Nancy's interest.

"I found that I really loved programming," she says. "Once I started, I thought this is what I wanted to do for the rest of my life."

She asked her teacher whether programming was worth pursuing as a career, if anybody would hire her. The teacher told her, "Come work for our company."

She joined the company as an assistant to a programmer, then realized she wanted to write programs herself. A friend steered her to a company that writes software for agricultural businesses such as farms and nurseries. She's been there more than five years, and her boss has given her great flexibility so that she can be home for her children. She comes to work at five in the morning and stays until one in the afternoon.

It has turned out to be a perfect life for her. "I have moments I crave being home with my children and making cookies," she says, "but I'm really lucky that I found my true calling." She also found a way to support herself and her children, and she's buying a new home for her family. "My confidence is way up from when my husband left me," she says. "It's incredible, the things I can do."

You might be sitting there with a lovely college degree from an extremely reputable college. And you might be able to parlay that excellent education into a perfectly fine job, but you also might find yourself in a position like Ellen's. She had taken a part-time job as a social worker, but she wanted to have a better job in the field, a full-time position that would give her more responsibility and the opportunity for promotion. When she knew that she wanted to make her job more important, she went back to school for a master's. "Going to school was the watershed," she says. "That's what made my work a commitment, a profession."

Still, there are no rules that say you have to know why you're going back to school. You don't have to have a specific goal in mind. Often that's the way we send our children to college. We encourage them to learn. Sure, we want them to be able to support themselves, to have some kind of work they can do. But don't we want them to be happy first? If we have a child who isn't driven toward a particular career, we steer them toward the liberal arts to enrich their minds and enable them to appreciate some of the nicer things in life. For many women who want to go back to college, that lack of exposure to whole parts of our global culture and history is what has pushed them into those hard little chairs with the desks on them.

That's how Elise happened to go back to college. She grew up in Kansas City and married at eighteen. College was not a tradition in her family. Success was moving to the suburbs, having four children two years apart, and doing volunteer work. Through volunteering her horizons began to expand. For the first time she saw what the outside world was like.

And when her husband took a new job on the East Coast, and the family relocated, her eyes were really opened. Without her support system of family and friends, and with her last child going off to kindergarten, she knew she'd be lonely and thought about taking courses. The school she picked was the one college in town she knew how to find.

Her expectations were limited, so initially she wasn't thinking in terms of a degree, but her husband, who had two advanced degrees, told her it would make sense to go for one. "I loved learning," she says. "Sometimes my kids and I did our homework together, or I'd go to bed right after they did, then get up at midnight and study until two." She enjoyed it so much that she got her bachelor's, then a master's in American literature. Then she started working on her doctorate.

All that education led to her first paying job, teaching English to middle-school students. "I didn't know curriculum or educational techniques, but I had children," says Elise. "I felt very grown-up finally. When I traveled to my first conference, I felt like a professional, not a mother."

Although she stayed in the job for twelve years, she had a feeling there was something else she could do, and she thought back to a writing course she had taken in college. "I never wanted to take the course," she recalls. "I didn't think I would get an A in it. Most women going back to college don't think they're doing well unless they're getting A's. You know, you feel you have to prove to everybody that your brain cells are not dead. And you're sure the school administrators are wondering why you're there wasting everyone's time if you're not great."

But the writing course changed her life. "I found a whole new aesthetic side that had been submerged." It's not submerged any longer. Today she's an author whose works are published in books and magazines. And she inspires other writers in the creative writing program she directs at a major university.

Did she ever think she could write this story? "Mine is a kind of fairy tale," she says.

Now what about those women who know *exactly* what they want to do? They do exist, you know, and they're able to make their dreams come true.

Helen Cooke had a very clear idea of how she wanted her life to go: newlywed to full-time mother at home to working mother. She kept to her plan. Until her son was born, she spent eight contented years in social work, becoming the director of a senior center. When she had little children, she stayed home with them for ten years to be able to breast-feed them, play with them, and experience them until they were more independent people ready to go off to school. Now, at forty-something, she's in the working-mother phase.

True to herself, Helen had her reentry carefully planned, too. She knew she wanted to go to school before going back to work because she didn't think she could get the kind of job in health and education for the elderly that she wanted without more education.

But this was not going to come from any ordinary college close to home. She looked around for a program and found one in England that had the exact curriculum she wanted. Her husband arranged for a year off, and they took their four-year-old and seven-year-old along. "We looked at it as our last fling before I entered into work full-time."

They spent a wonderful year abroad. Says Helen, "Going back to school gave me confidence and updated me. I got a marketable skill that was like money in the bank."

When she got home, she wasn't sure exactly how to find that perfect job, and she turned to the classified ads. "What an education," says Helen. "It's very hard to tell what the job is. One day I saw an ad for a health consultant for the elderly. I thought, 'That job has my name on it. They can't possibly hire anyone else. No one could be as qualified.' I had to apply.

"Then I had cold feet. Was I ready to go after ten years? How could I make child-care arrangements? My daughter was going to kindergarten. Would she need me? Then I figured I would just do it. So I applied and never heard a word! After a while I saw the ad again. So they hadn't filled it. I was so confident I would get it. I applied again, and they hired me. It's a great job, and I love it.

"I'm glad my life has worked out this way. Do my children know now at ten and twelve that their mother was home when they were three and four? I hope so. But I really did it for myself."

Opening your mind to all that school has to offer is a wonderful experience. And it can lead you to understand that you are capable of more than you ever thought possible. That's the story of Ann.

As the services of a big hospital in a not-so-great big-city neighborhood became more and more sophisticated, the administrators thought it was time they gave something of value to their neighborhood, since part of the hospital's mission was a commitment to the community. When they felt the pain from their nursing shortage, they recognized that they could look to the neighborhood for some talent to tap.

They found lots of mothers out there—mothers who were on welfare, mothers who hadn't finished high school, mothers who were single and dependent on public assistance, mothers who just needed a job. The hospital administrators decided the best thing they could do for everybody would be to make these mothers better providers by training them to be practical nurses.

And why not? These mothers had been developing their skills for years with their own families. The hospital developed a training and placement program that assesses the academic skills of women who wish to enroll, then sends them back to a cooperating community college if they need more work or on to practical nursing training if they're ready.

One of those women good and ready was Ann. "Once I had thought I would always be home," she says. "I always felt there was a tradition in mothers being home with children, that I wouldn't be a good mother if I were working. But we've been pushed to the limit financially, and I had to do something to keep my six kids in Catholic school. The economy has changed our lives.

"My husband was the first one who said I should go to work. But I didn't know what I could do. I already felt like a failure at running the house. It took one hundred and fifty percent of my effort to do what people do naturally. I never was a fabulous cook. It's not that I didn't try. I kept the house clean, but it took everything out of me. I have sisters who are cleaning fanatics. I always looked at my kids and said, 'Heck, I'll take 'em to the playground instead.'

"I'd always loved learning and did well in school, but as one of eleven kids it was better for me to be working and take the burden off my parents. I really, really missed that education.

"I wondered what I could be trained for. A teacher, a hairdresser? I'd always wanted to go into nursing, except nursing school was full-time. Then I heard about this practical-nursing program for mothers. I *had* to get in and almost flipped out when I thought I didn't.

"My mind was like a sponge when I went to school. I wished I had done it before, but I probably wouldn't have appreciated it if I had. Age is the great equalizer. In my early twenties, people intimidated me. Being forty now is liberating.

"The time I had to wait was not wasted time. It made me a strong person. It's how I see patients. The young nurses around me haven't got their knocks in life and can't sympathize. Some patients are debilitated. They have bad odors or get agitated. Being older and having gone through a lot, I understand. I've seen ups and downs in my life. And I know I'll be there someday, too. Every one of my patients was somebody's baby. If they're upset, I just think they're having a bad day. I learned that being a mother."

Ann wants to become a registered nurse. But her husband can look even beyond that. Not long ago he told her, "Ann, I wish I had money. I would send you to medical school."

You can convince anybody that "Mother" on your resume means contractor, comptroller, purchasing agent, personnel manager, judge, corrections officer, and tenured professor.

Even though you're probably fond of shouting to the heavens, "With all I do, I could run General Motors!" nobody's going to buy it. They look at you and see you're a mom, so you're expected to do all that. Unfortunately, you and the other moms are the only ones who realize you've actually been running a business all these years.

So let's turn those eight zillion marketable skills into something that looks good on paper. Career counselor Vicki Kramer knows just what you've been going through. "Women who have been at home always say to me, 'I haven't been doing anything valuable. I have no current skills.' Really, they tend to undervalue their skills.

"They talk as if they were locked up in a house for years doing nothing. But when I ask questions, I can find out that one was constantly redecorating, one was heavily involved in school activities, and another did every volunteer activity there is. That's a lot."

And if they think they've just been at home with their kids, what does that mean? "I ask what they did with their kids," says Kramer. "Maybe the kids were very sports-oriented, and the mother had to be in so many places, driving to practices and games. That shows me she is incredibly organized. That's an important skill."

One woman came to her thinking she had done nothing. Probing her, Kramer found out she had built a new house. Essentially, she had been a contractor. So she put her resume in very professional terms. She wrote it as an essay. She sold her managerial skills and her knowledge of all these different areas.

She discussed everything from her budget to her family's needs and all the decisions she had to make. It worked. She found a job.

Ellie had done important volunteer work in California, organizing voters and legislators on key environmental issues. "Volunteering is not just licking stamps," she says. "Managing a group of one hundred volunteers is not an easy task." She was able to change her volunteer job into a full-paying one.

And Eleanor, who went back to work as an author escort in Houston, is most impressed with the mothers she meets from her children's school. "These women are tremendous organizers," she says. "They raised seventy thousand dollars at a silent auction, and this is a public school. We have the best playground equipment you ever saw. If you could extrapolate all the skills they're putting in here to a career out there, they'd be really successful. I'm positive that a mother who runs a household can do anything. It's just like running a business."

See, I told you. Now *you* have to believe it. When you go out to sell yourself to a potential employer, you have to be confident. Trust your talents. Go after what you want. Convince that person that you are the one and only person for the job.

If you've been home, you're not going to lose the work skills you've developed, either. A lot of jobs have core skills of communicating, organizing, planning, analyzing, and team playing. Being with your children keeps your skills in play, not at the bottom of the toy box.

Alice even found these skills to be a selling point. She went back to a law practice after being home with her children for eight years. Ten years after that, she decided to run for judge. "When I first ran for office," says Alice, "everyone asked, 'Do you think a woman can control a courtroom?'

"'After three children,' I'd tell them, 'I think a courtroom would be a piece of cake'"

———

Are you wondering how you're going to muster this kind of self-confidence? Confused about how to tell a skill from a habit? When somebody tells you to apply what you've learned being a mother at home does your classroom notebook look blank?

You can boost your self-confidence and make it seem as though this assurance comes naturally to you. Take a hard look at what you've accomplished with your volunteer work, your spouse, your children, your home. List what you're proud of, the tangible things you've done.

Don't put yourself down or assume that you're just a mom and you've been out of the workforce too long. Turn the situation around. Your experience has done a lot for you. Realize, too, that you can stretch yourself. Be ready to take on new tasks. Imagine how you might be able to translate your talents. And always assume that you're going to end up on top.

No matter what kind of job you're considering, you can make the best of any situation. Isn't that what you've done at home? Look how your hard work paid off with your family. That should build your confidence.

And it might help you to join a support group such as FEMALE or Mothers At Home. There's probably a group near you. These moms help you find the best in yourself. Heidi Brennan had a career in health-care management. Now she's spokesperson of Mothers At Home in Virginia. "I felt stupid when I came home," she says. "I was falling into the trap of believing that perfect dusting is a measure of your worth. When I worked I could read three newspapers a day. With babies it was impossible. I learned time management so I don't struggle and feel bad about myself. Now I scan the paper. I keep up with the world. I'm in touch."

It's only when you feel positive about the job you're doing at home and put it in perspective that you are ready to look for a job. That's when you can determine your strengths.

And then you just might be ready to put "Mother" on your resume.

———

Janelle had never finished college and was nervous about applying as an older woman with children. She was faced with college applications that had big blanks for essays about leadership and future plans. She was apprehensive about being compared to accomplished high school seniors when she'd only been home with her children. But one day when she was working on her applications, she had a great realization. "I really had done something at home. I made big decisions about my children's futures, their schooling, their medical care. I had far more autonomy and responsibility than many people who hold paying jobs. This stuff was really important.

"For my application essay I wrote about my leadership capabilities with my daughter's Brownie troop and said that my troops were never lost or under duress. I used my ability to fix broken drains to demonstrate my ingenuity. And for meeting challenges I told about my marathon running, that my determination made up for what I lacked in physical talent. I was a mother. This kind of application was my survival tactic."

Of course she got in.

When Adair wanted to convince a restaurant owner to hire her to cook in his restaurant, she decided to put together a resume. She had worked at church bazaars and catering for friends for years, but to distinguish herself she put her five children on her resume. She caught his attention. "He thought it was very funny. No one had ever done this before. I got the job, and my children went to work there."

It's happening more and more. Recently, a California woman running for Congress listed "mother" in the space in which candidates can enter their occupation on the ballot. The state didn't recognize that profession, but the acting secretary of state thought the law should be changed. The secretary allowed, "That piece of information might be important in a voter's decision." Or an employer's.

Part of being smart about knowing where to apply your talents is understanding the job market. You hear about the information superhighway and feel like you're on a dirt road while your three-year-old is already computer-literate. Keep up with the news, read the magazines and papers. There are always stories about trends in the workplace.

Certainly, the stories about downsizing, cost-cutting, and

outsourcing can make your breath come in short gasps and send you back under the covers for a week. But you have to read between the lines and find the positive news there. Yes, we have turned into a service economy. And, lady, you've been serving for several years. You're good at that. And if you don't have to go to work to provide the only income for your family, you don't have to have a huge job that pays a fortune.

Among the twenty-five hottest careers for women, according to *Working Woman* magazine, are computer programmer, telecommunications manager, employee trainer, family physician, nurse-practitioner, physical therapist, diversity manager, ombudsman, environmental consultant, private investigator, and professional-temp placement specialist.

Some of these might sound overwhelming to you now. But if they interest you, start out by volunteering in one of these areas or help out in someone's office. It gives you a chance to demonstrate your skills in a real situation. Take a course or two to learn more and see if you like it. Often when you want to go back to work, you have to learn new skills.

Advocacy groups for working women are not entirely thrilled with this list because most of the jobs do nothing for breaking the glass ceiling, putting women on corporate boards, or eliminating the double standard in salaries, but that doesn't mean one of these jobs might not be right for you.

Find out which corporations are recognized for encouraging working women. You'll get some help from Catalyst, a working women's advocacy and research organization that annually awards companies who meet their strict criteria for promoting the leadership of women. Corporations recognized lately include Pitney Bowes, Motorola, and McDonald's.

Then find women who are doing the job you want to do and learn from them. Yes, you do know how to find them. "It's just like finding a plumber," says Options founder Vicki Kramer. "Call everybody you know. Get names and suggestions, then call people you don't know. Somebody will see you."

"A lot of returning mothers come to see me," says Joanne, a banker in New York who stayed home when her children were young. "They usually come through a mutual friend. They don't know about employment agencies or don't trust them. And these women don't answer classified ads because they usually ask for experience, and these women do a lot better with an interview. The women I'm interested in are those who have a clear sense of what they're good at."

Decisiveness is difficult at the beginning of the job search. It's hard to specify the exact job you want. One woman told Joanne she was good at sales because she had been in charge of projects and fund-raising at her church. "Talking to her, I learned something more concrete," says Joanne. "She had been bored and started selling a line of toys from her home. It didn't involve a lot of money, but that's what told me she could sell." Eventually, she got a job in branch banking. "If she's good, she'll move up quickly. I'd say a couple of years."

You also need to know what you want to get out of your job. Career counselors will tell you that there are many reasons to work. Aside from money, some of the most important include being able to use your skills and talents, keeping yourself marketable, and contributing to your society.

Many jobs or careers can be defined by the particular attributes that you need to do them. "Decide where you get your greatest satisfaction," Vicki Kramer advises, "whether it's from being responsible as a manager for total results, working independently, starting your own business, being confident that your paycheck is coming from a secure employer, designing your work life around your current social and family life, or going out on a limb."

When Shirley Bressler's two daughters were grown, she wanted a job with flexible hours and independence "so that I could run my own store," she says. "I knew that selling residential real estate would be perfect for me. I talked to a number of people in the business until I knew I wanted to go with this specific job and this specific company. I met with my future manager during a blizzard on a Sunday. Monday I had the job and was in the office."

Take enough time deciding what you want to do so that you don't meet with failures. Don't go after the wrong thing.

Anna is a school administrator who often interviews mothers who want to go back to work. "A lot of women come to see me because they think they can teach young children. When I ask their qualifications, they say, 'I'm a mother. My children are in high school. I know how to deal with children.'

"Then I ask how they would teach a young child to read, and they have no answer. They don't understand the amount of formal training that elementary teachers have. A lot of these mothers would do better to go to the high school or community college to teach. There the technique isn't quite so critical." True, mothers who are artisans or interested in any particular field could sell their talents to community colleges and teach courses.

On the other hand, Anna welcomes mothers who had taught before their children were born and want to return to teaching. She knows just what they learned at home, since she had taken time off herself. "Being home gave me an idea of all that children could do. I have a dyslexic child, and that helped me have more empathy in dealing with parents. At home I discovered that children are capable of so much if given a chance. They respond so much to encouragement."

Many employers will regard your having worked before as a bonus. "It's easier to hire a woman who knows what the working world is about," says a banker in New York. "She knows about commitments, being someplace on time, rolling up her sleeves and getting work done. If a woman has learned all this at twenty-two, it's better than trying to teach it to her at forty-two."

Gina was able to go back to the work she'd done before. She left her job as a chemical engineer at Du Pont when she was pregnant with her first child because, as she says, "In the seventies, there was no flexible anything."

She kept her hand in as a consultant since she knew she'd go back someday, but she mostly spent her days involved with her children, her community, and her church.

Du Pont tendered a couple of offers, but they were full-time or nothing, and she wasn't ready until her youngest was in school. So after a ten-year hiatus, Gina went back in through the personnel department. She filled out forms, had interviews, and was offered a job in two months.

"Not much had changed," she observes, "except that the computers got smaller and easier to use. I'd been reading about my field. If you can do something, why would you forget it?"

She learned a lot at home, too. "I found that building a hundred million dollar chemical plant is a lot easier than planning your children's summers."

M any women who are at home with their children feel that if they return to the workforce without a real career—you know, that important title and big expense account—they're not really successful working mothers. They think others will make fun of their jobs, that's it not even worth it to put out the effort. Not so.

The division between job and career is not so clear. It's mostly a function of your own attitude. Vicki Kramer says, "A career presumes that there is some growth and development going on. It requires the mind-set of a commitment. What matters here is what you want to accomplish at this point in your life."

"*Career* sounds very yuppie," says Heidi Brennan. "Is processing chickens a career or a job? We're a country of hobbyists. Spend your time doing what you like. A traditional career like marketing and computer programming might not light your fire like square dancing does. So turn square dancing into your career."

If you've gone back to school and invested lots of money in

education and training, you're going to look at your work as your career. That's because you're ready to accept that you'll be successful, and you're committed to a goal. Once again, think about what you've learned at home. Your goal is to make your children confident and work up to their potential and find their particular niche. Now be understanding, compassionate, and patient with yourself.

Still, you might go back to work just because you need a job and then find that your innate talents and mother-learned skills will turn your job into your *career*—your whole new identity. That's what happened to Joyce.

Joyce faced a horrible abyss when she was widowed at forty-four. She had $180,000 in unpaid medical bills, a malpractice suit, no pension or benefits, absolutely no income. Of course, with three children she had to find work near her home in the Los Angeles suburbs of Orange County. "But I was so depressed," she says, "I didn't want to go back to work. I hated to turn the doorknob in my house. Where would I even go? Where was a place for me? I thought it would be better if I weren't alive."

She turned to a friend who sent her out the door and into a job. She worked sixteen hours a week at minimum wage coordinating volunteers at the hospital where her husband had been a doctor.

"Slowly, my confidence was coming back," says Joyce, and she applied for a better job as assistant to a senior analyst of the psychiatry department of the medical school. "I told my friends that if I had a breakdown, at least I'd be working for a psychiatrist."

Joyce was amazed to find her potential new boss was a woman who was a lot younger than she. She was a career person with a big job and small child. But she was sympathetic, and Joyce decided to be open and honest with her.

"I said I believed I could do the job, that even though I didn't have the experience I was willing to learn, that I would work extra hours and take less money. She gave me a chance because I laid myself open to her.

"I bit my tongue a lot. I did what I was told. I became like a mom to her and kept her organized. Whenever she'd say, 'Joyce, can you do this for me?' I always did.

"I was very patient in this job. I knew I wasn't an authority at work. If you're middle-aged and going for a job, the odds are your boss is going to be younger than you. You have to listen and learn. The way you would do something is probably old-fashioned."

After she'd been able to prove herself, Joyce's boss sent her to the library to help with research, and by the time there was a department fund-raiser, Joyce had the confidence to make suggestions "because it reminded me of helping with the Girl Scouts or raising money for the football team."

Eventually, her boss recommended Joyce as project coordinator for an organ-donor group. She learned to deal with the coroner's office and law enforcement and medical students. One day she was in a conversation about work with two women doctors when a male doctor came up to the group and said, "We need you to speak at our state conference."

"I looked around to see who he was talking to," Joyce recalls. "I realized it was me. I was the authority. I agreed to give the speech. And although I almost vomited before I went up to the podium, I was confident I knew my material. It felt really great. On the inside and the outside."

Sometimes the person who needs the most convincing of your talents is you.

Maybe you're one of those people who has always dreamed of having your own business. Your friends tell you you're a great baker, a great cook, a great knitter, a great seamstress, a great party planner, a great Little League coach, a great fund-raiser. It takes an extraordinary commitment. When Vicki Kramer started Options she went into business with a partner because she didn't want to have to make all these new decisions alone. They liked the idea that they could grow the business as fast or slowly as they wanted to. And they both thought they could work part-time. "Were we crazy!" Vicki says. "Sometimes you have no freedom at all. You never put your own business to bed. And once you have employees, you have their welfare to worry about, too."

It's a fallacy that starting your own business is an easy way to go back to work or the way to get rich quick. Before you do it you have to consider how much of a risk taker you are and whether you can be independently motivated or you need the atmosphere of a big organization.

Starting that cute little restaurant is a favorite fantasy for many women, but the amount of time and money involved can be formidable. Adair always wanted to start a restaurant in Boston, but when she told her family she wanted to open her own place, they said, "Guess that means no more vacations."

"I love the idea," Adair says, "but I don't want to work that hard. I know that restaurants that really work are ones the owners are in all the time."

If you have the courage, the energy, and the dream to be an entrepreneur, you can make it work the way Carol Ray has done.

She always knew she wanted to go into her own business, but she didn't want to do it while her son was growing up. She wanted to be very involved with his education. While he was young, she worked as a teacher to have a schedule compatible with his, but she always kept her dream of going into her own business alive by selling jewelry, cookware, and cosmetics out of her house.

Then, after her son was out of college and on his own, and when she heard that a big old building on North Broad Street in Philadelphia—the Blue Horizon—was for sale, she jumped for it.

It's one thing for a woman to buy her own building and another for a woman to buy a legendary boxing venue. Carol never saw it that way. The Blue Horizon had enough rooms to use for parties, dances, bingo, and concerts, too, which would enrich the neighborhood, and she saw boxing as a way to pay her rent. She marveled at the Blue Horizon's cherry-wood paneling and stained-glass skylights. She acknowledged the leaky pipes, crumbling chimney, and deteriorated roof. Undefeated, she figured out how to get the $550,000 to buy it.

First she went to banks. "They don't want to help women or minorities go into business, I'm convinced of it," Carol Ray says. "They'd tell me I needed collateral, just like any man who wanted to come in and get money to start a business. 'If I had collateral,' I said, 'I wouldn't be having this conversation with you.'"

She crisscrossed the state for three years, calling on minority development groups, community developers, politicians, and private businesspeople for help. In the meantime, she took on two partners who were extremely supportive and complemented her visionary talents. "I learned to be able to read whether people believed in what I was saying," she says. "And I decided only to talk to people who would encourage me."

When they finally got the loans and had closed the deal, Carol was left with thirty-five hundred dollars to run the business. "It was insanity. I should have put my head on my dining-room table and sobbed." But there was no time for that because a Philadelphia judge ordered major repairs such as a new roof, new chimney, catwalk renovations, and a new fire alarm to be completed before their first boxing match coming up in nine days.

She found workers to come in and get it all done. "I know they were here because they were amazed and proud that three African-Americans would take on this venture of making the Blue Horizon a center for the community," she says. In the few years she and her partners have owned the Blue Horizon, they've faced more repairs, but they've also opened a new party room, they put on a concert featuring Boyz II Men when they were still a neighborhood singing group, and now they're planning bingo.

And the boxing matches go on. Today you'll find Carol behind the counter serving hot dogs and sodas to the elegantly suited businesspeople who jam the Blue Horizon on fight nights. But you'll also find her reading about her heroes like Don King, Bill Gates, and Donald Trump. "They faced the same kinds of problems I have," she says. "I know I'm going to make it big."

No matter how many millions you've volunteered to raise for others, it makes a difference when it's going into your own checking account.

Okay, find your place over there with the rest of the mothers.

Now, if you think that you should be paid the going rate, you know, the one that gets calculated every once in a while by some think tank that tells you how much money a mother at home should make, step forward.

(A chorus of giant steps is heard.)

Fine. But what's the grumbling about? Not enough money for twenty-four hours a day, seven days a week? It's probably not.

But let's face it. All the men in the world will have to have the capability to get pregnant, administer liquid Tylenol without spilling, compile a list of eighteen possible baby-sitters and actually book one for a Saturday night before you will *ever* be paid to stay home and take care of your children.

We do this out of love, folks. And moms don't make their kids put quarters in every twenty minutes. Although a few thank-yous, pleases, sweet little kisses, and I love yous don't hurt.

Even though these days it is quite acceptable, even fashionable, to praise mothers at home, to acknowledge that their work is very important and worthwhile and to honor their choice to be with their children, there's no escaping the fact that praise doesn't pay the mortgage. Or the college tuitions.

Creeping up on you, are they? Pushing you back to work?

Money is a big reason that many mothers return to work. But you know what? You're going to get an unexpected bonus with your first paycheck. A new sense of self-respect.

Think of how good your children feel when you pay them to do jobs around the house. It changes things. When you have a job, suddenly you're working hard, getting feedback and a paycheck. It's gratifying.

Samantha never had to worry about money when she was growing up in the suburbs of Chicago. Her parents sent her off to Mount Holyoke College, she married a boy from a fine family, and they had three lovely children. But, as Samantha says, "Our house was nicer than our friends' houses. I didn't have to do anything to it. I didn't even have the pleasure of renovating. I sat there with nothing to do."

She began volunteering for different organizations and had help a couple of days a week to stay with her children so she could do this. She really wanted a job. She'd always been interested in business and stocks and had made the investment decisions in her family. She told her husband she wanted to be a stockbroker. It seemed a logical step.

"You can't be a stockbroker," he told her. "You might lose money for people."

"I should have divorced him then. Instead I waited ten years."

She went to her father, who published a magazine about local commercial real estate and asked him whether she could write a column about women in the business.

"There aren't any," he said to her.

"I'll find them, and you won't have to pay me much to do it," Samantha said. That convinced him.

Samantha found a group called Women in Construction as her starting point. "I loved my new identity as a working woman," she says.

She started to think bigger and wanted a job in which she could make twenty thousand dollars a year, her absolute goal. She had a new husband, and now she was going to be a stockbroker. In 1982 when the Dow Jones average was around 700, she walked into a big brokerage house and met the boss. "I thought he looked familiar, and it turned out that as a volunteer I had checked him into a charity luncheon. He knew I had raised money and sold program advertising for the event. He told me, 'If you can raise that kind of money, you can be a good stockbroker.'" Even though she had no license, he gave her a draw of twenty thousand dollars.

The stock market began to take off. Samantha returned to her old contacts at Women in Construction, who gave her their whole pension plan to invest. Some of the women gave her their personal accounts. One of her biggest clients came because she, as the neophyte in the suburban office, had to sit near the door to handle walk-ins. A man who came through the door gave her his personal multimillion-dollar account to invest. Sure, she was lucky to get the account, "but I was also able to pick the stocks and make the account grow," she says.

It took a while for her boss to understand how smart she was. When she was hired, he announced at a sales meeting that through her father and her two husbands, Samantha knew everybody in town. Naturally, she says, "All the brokers hated me and thought I would take away all their clients."

After a few months, when she'd made some good investments, a top-producing broker in another office wanted to hire her and pay her fifty thousand dollars a year. She didn't take the job, but in her first year she ended up making more than that.

In a business that is all about money, Samantha knows what it means to her. "As I've made money, I have learned that success is more than numbers. I've built up trust in my clients over the years. As long as you don't lose and show you're doing it not just to make a buck at their expense, you'll do well. Many of my client relationships have become very close. I'm dealing with a person's future, their whole life. I might have all their money. I have to be knowledgeable and honest and do what's best for my client, and it might not be where I make the most money.

"Certainly, the money I have made and my position have given me confidence and a whole new identity in my community. I am still volunteering, but now I do it as a businesswoman. It makes a difference to me."

Some women's husbands find it difficult when they go back, worrying that the comfortable life as they know it will change completely. Anna knew her husband felt like that. He didn't really want her to return to her job as a teacher in a girls' school. She says, "When I first went back to work, I wasn't making a great deal of money. We didn't have enough for a housekeeper, and the kids were old enough that I didn't need to pay for baby-sitters. But all the housework was more than I could handle. My biggest mistake was trying to be Supermom. I stopped paying much attention to all that. And I kind of left my husband alone at night, too, while I graded papers.

"After the first year, he asked me with trepidation, 'Are you going back next year?' I told him that yes, I was, and that the family could help me out.

"During the second year we all got used to it. At the end of the year, he asked, 'You *are* going back next year, aren't you?'

"'Why? Are you enjoying the check?' It had come to be very helpful.

"'That, and you just seem a lot happier,' he said. And he was right."

When Peggy went into teaching at a middle school in Washington, she was surprised by how much the money meant to her. "My husband had supported me for many years before I went to work," says Peggy. "When I started making it myself, the money was no small thing. The amount wasn't big, but it made my job seem more important. I had done a lot of volunteer work, and now someone thought enough to *pay* me for what I did."

She decided to have her own bank account and her own savings. She pays a share of the household expenses. "The money has also given me an independence I never had," she says. "I wasn't always able to buy gifts, pay for household help, and buy my own clothing without anybody protesting."

With five daughters, Adair Burlingham, on the other hand, knew not only why she wanted money but also what it would do for her. "In 1957 I could have written a book called *100 Ways to Make an Extra $1,000 a Year*." She drove a school bus and a taxi in Boston. Since she liked to cook, she started a little catering business. And since she picked events like school and church bazaars, she only made two hundred dollars a year from the catering.

Moneymaking became more serious when her marriage fell apart. Her kids were between five and fourteen years old, and her husband wasn't interested in paying her much alimony. "It was the late sixties, and I was dying to work in one of these hippie restaurants in Boston where we lived," she says. "I didn't know how to get a job. At thirty-seven, I was too embarrassed to ask for a job at one of these places because everyone there was so young."

When she heard about a job as a cook at a restaurant she liked, she made an appointment with the owner. He hired her to work one night a week. Adair remembers, "I just loved it, and I was making money. Once I got that paycheck, I thought I was *really* a good cook. It gave me confidence and independence." She stayed at the restaurant fourteen years, then went on to teach classes and cook for other restaurants. She's recently retired from another restaurant. "But I'm not finished working," she notes. "I started going to a course called 'Old Wine in New Bottles: Career Changes at Midlife.'"

The need for money strikes no one like it does a recently divorced woman. No matter what kind of settlement she has, it probably hasn't been negotiated out of the generosity and kind-hearted spirit of her spouse. Most likely, she's going to have to go to work. New York divorce attorney Harriet Newman Cohen spends every single day thinking about the plight of divorced women. A self-made millionaire, she didn't start working until after she'd been home with her children—and until after her marriage broke up.

She was nineteen when she got married in the early fifties and went to college to be a Latin professor. Even though she went for her master's, she didn't think women should work and stayed home with her four children, becoming active in the schools and the neighborhood.

Her marriage wasn't great. Her husband busied himself with

his own activities and would leave the family at home to take ski trips on his own. The divisions deepened as Harriet realized they had different values. "He didn't understand money at all. I thought that if we had some money, we should spend it on schools for the kids. He wanted to spend it on his ski vacation. Unofficially, he walked out, leaving me with four kids and a housekeeper."

She had to let the housekeeper go, of course, and go to work as a math teacher. "It wore me out emotionally and physically. Every day I would limp out of the classroom."

She had some close lawyer friends, who observed that she had the personality to be a lawyer. At that time law schools were beginning to open their doors to women. Her four kids now ranged in age from seven to seventeen, and she thought being a lawyer might be a good way to make a living.

"I told my husband I wanted to go to law school. He, naturally, thought it was a bad idea. I took the law boards, and then, according to his wishes, I waited a year to see if I still wanted to go."

Of course she did, but she was nervous. "I was thirty-eight and felt like a hundred and eight. How could I go to school with these young boys? I decided I would swallow hard and do it."

Her mother was not supportive either. "It's not your turn," she said. "It's the children's turn."

Harriet answered, "We'll take this turn together."

"Your husband will never stay with you," she warned Harriet.

"Well, if he's really going to leave me," Harriet told her, "I better get educated."

He left her two weeks before final exams in her second year.

He took one suitcase. Harriet told him, "We're not going to be all right."

He answered, "You're going to be fine."

"Hah," she says. "We had no money. It was very rough. I worked as hard as I could in school. I had to do it for my kids. I was terrified that if I didn't make law review, I would never get a job. So I made it."

Interestingly, of the 10 percent of her class who were women, every one of them was a returning mother. Each one of them has had a distinguished career in the law. Harriet notes that two of her dearest women friends from law school had much stronger marriages after going through all this. "Change does not rock or break a good marriage," she says.

"When I graduated I felt terrific. The boys didn't look like kids to me anymore. It all seemed to disappear. It was probably good training because I knew I was going to have to go out and work for younger people. I felt like a kid myself going for interviews. I projected the image of a young graduate who would fit right in any situation. I didn't perceive my baggage as a problem, just as my situation."

She set out to be a generalist, maybe a litigator, but found she was awfully good at matrimonial law. Not surprising, since she had lived through it.

"The reason I've done well is that I understand that as the lawyer I'm the protector of these children and their mother," she says. "I do what it takes to help them. I try to get them money, not take it from them.

"When I represent a dependent wife, I have to advocate that she's damaged merchandise. It's a tension for me. The husband, attorneys, and judge think she is going to walk out of the house completely disempowered and displaced and be motivated to find herself and go to work. The sense is that a divorced woman will get recycled. She is supposed to be reconstituted into a different form.

"I always tell these dependent women, 'You can earn a living. You turned out a magnificent family. You can be magnificent, too.'"

When it comes down to the practical matter of asking for money, most of us wish we could get somebody else to do it. Negotiating for yourself and understanding your worth in cold cash is difficult. It can make you very nervous to ask for a salary.

Look at what you need now and what you'll need in the future. Do you need benefits? Do you have a retirement fund? What do you care about accomplishing? Is a big salary your important goal?

Figure out your realistic money needs. Write it all down, or get a computer program. What are your monthly bills? Taxes? Insurance? What do you need for emergencies? Tuitions? This is not as impossible as it sounds. Most women at home control the family finances already. You've probably been involved in planning, and the notion that women don't know a thing about money doesn't apply to you.

A career counselor can start you off with a salary idea. You're going to have to talk to people in your field. They'll tell you how much you can reasonably expect to make. Professional associations can be helpful, too, because they do salary searches.

When I went back to work as a freelance advertising writer,

I had no idea how much to ask for. I had always worked for an annual salary. Starting out, I was so grateful for work I took whatever money was offered. When I decided to be more businesslike, I asked other writers what they got, and they told me how to set up my own fee structure. It made my life a lot easier. And I didn't feel so sheepish when I asked for money.

———

Another factor to consider is compromise. Are you going to accept less money because it means that you'll work fewer hours and can be with your family? Where do you want the emphasis to be?

You do make trade-offs when you go back to work. You can't always have the best of all possible worlds, but what is second best? "I always thought that I wouldn't go back to work unless I could have the best," says Sue, who went back to work in her husband's business. "I wanted the Bahamas, not the local beach. I was sitting and doing nothing, just complaining how I couldn't make enough to bother to go back. I've made trade-offs in terms of salary, but I can have the work schedule I want to be with my children after school."

Mary Ann Sharpe went back to work as a French teacher in Long Island, New York, when her first child was born, and she spent nearly half her income on child care. It wasn't a problem because she and her husband were still able to bank half her net pay. By the time she had two more children, things were out of control. She had barely anything left after paying for child care. It didn't make sense for her to continue working, so she left her job.

Recently, though, things changed. The director of the private school where she worked called and told her that during the time she had been at home, they had added a nursery school where she could send two of her daughters. She decided to go back to work there between twelve and three and send her kids to the nursery school there. "It's nice that I can bring them with me," says Mary Ann. "Their tuition is mostly covered. I have it deducted from my paycheck. Normally, I would not send my children here. It's very expensive. Now I get the best of everything.

"My salary isn't huge. It's not changing my lifestyle too much, but it helps. I do feel better when I'm working. I'm a mother half-time and a teacher half-time." She's planning to change directions once her daughters are in school all day and go back for a master's degree—very slowly, one course at a time.

"Eventually, I'll make some money," she says. "Many of my friends have young children, and we're plotting now so we can go back. I can't afford to stay home forever. Besides, I see a value in working. If I'm not going to be home with my children, I'm going to do something significant."

Yes, money sends most of us into the workforce, but remember that you aren't less of a person if you're making less than a fortune.

Helen Cooke searched a long time for that perfect job. She had to make money, but she also had to be happy. She'd grown up seeing her mother working two jobs and her father working split shifts. "I knew they were just working for the money. It was unsatisfying. I didn't see my husband doing that. He loves his job. I wanted to love mine, too. That's why I decided to be picky.

"The kind of public-service job I was interested in is not the kind you make big bucks in. Coming to terms with that was important. Otherwise, I would always be miserable. I knew from the beginning that you work for an awful long time. You want to feel good about yourself and what you do."

Now that you've nurtured the dreams of everybody else, it's their turn to encourage yours.

Is it genetic for mothers to utter the mantra, "Of course you can do it, of course you can do it," until they're hypnotized into thinking their child should play professional sports, go to Harvard on a full scholarship, be the most popular person who ever went to school, do headstands, have neat handwriting, and even make a bed every once in a while?

It must be.

How else could we be completely blind to their inability to slam-dunk, land an overhead smash, or comprehend calculus?

And why do we continue to straighten their rooms even though Mrs. Piggle Wiggle tells us not to?

We know deep down what our children can do. We know it better than *they* do. As mothers, we're awestruck by the miracles of our children. But we're never, ever surprised. We know they have it in them.

How would you like somebody to feel this way about you, right this minute, when you want to come in with a food processor and chop up every neat little ingredient of your life?

Not that you need anyone to tell you this, but you're probably going to have to launch an aggressive sales campaign to explain the merits of your next life stage and why you need the assistance of those who depend upon you to note and sponsor both the grandest events and simplest blips of their lives. That complete, unquestioned devotion is not going to come naturally. But it's great when you've got it. No matter how you get it.

Often it takes some time before family members realize that they can not only adapt but also benefit when Mom returns to work.

When Margaret went to work, her family adjusted quite nicely, much to their surprise. "I remember the children complaining a lot more about my being a volunteer," she says. "I would always say, 'Mommy can't talk to you now. I'm busy planning the board meeting.' That drove my kids crazy. But when I went to work, they began to do things at home. Two of my children became good cooks, and another learned to do laundry. The oldest never learned this stuff but did a lot of grocery shopping. There was a lot of control involved, and they liked it."

Anna found the same truth. "I got someone to clean the

house when I first went back to teaching," she says. "When the children were older I thought we could save the money and they could help me clean. By the time they were in high school, they did their own washing and made their own lunches. When my daughter first came home from college, she said, 'Mom, you can't believe the kids who don't know how to put things in washing machines.' My children felt that they were important to the running of the house. Some mothers don't feel it's necessary, but it made me a lot happier."

Happy Fernandez, a Philadelphia city councilwoman, was never crazy about taking care of the household duties, but when she began her political work, she had less time to do it all.

"Since I wasn't so interested in the house," she says, "my two older boys had to learn to pick up their stuff."

By the time her third son was born, she had already gone back to work, and the household stuff was too much for her. She was crying one day when her husband asked her what the problem was.

"I can't handle it all," she told him.

"What do you hate the most?" he asked.

"I can't wash another diaper," she replied.

"Okay," he answered, then took their oldest son aside and delegated the responsibility to him.

$\sim$

Many of the husbands have a tough time at first. But you have to understand that many of them did not grow up with mothers who worked and they're not yet comfortable with *your* working. You have to encourage them and pat them on the back, too.

Lisa returned to her old law firm as an attorney when her daughter was in prekindergarten. "She was small enough for a few years that she didn't need much extra doing and driving. When she got a little older, and there was soccer practice and the like, I asked my husband to pitch in. He still didn't have a great amount of respect for my work since it was part-time, but when I was elected to the school board, he got a lot better. Psychologically, it was easier for him to do more when I said I had to be at a school-board meeting. He thinks it's important, and he encourages me to do it."

When Dena went to law school, then to work in a firm, she knew that in the early years she would have to put in long hours on the job. "My husband was very supportive of all that I did," she says, "but he naturally assumed that I would still be keeping a lot of those wife roles. He's the president of his company, and when we go to big parties or sales meetings, he still expects me to coach him on the names of every man, woman, and child, plus plan cocktail parties and go on outings with the wives. He was raised in another era. My marriage is important to me, so I'm going to do it."

Some husbands can be very understanding of your reasons for going to work and offer their support in subtle ways. That's what Peach Harbold found when she became a truck driver.

"Society made me feel guilty for not working," says Peach. "I felt I wasn't contributing. I was just the ultimate room mother."

Her husband drove a truck, so he was always gone, and she had to handle everything with her four children. "By the time the last one left home here in central Pennsylvania, I was a basket case. I wanted to do something, but I didn't have any sort of talent or training. I thought I wasn't good for a whole lot. My friends said I was such a good mother and cook, but I didn't want to be remembered for being a good cook."

Her husband and she had always planned that when the kids were grown they'd be out in the truck together. So they started doing that. Since they weren't used to being together for those thirty years, riding together was quite eye-opening.

"We found out a lot about each other. Luckily, we liked each other. One day he was tired and pulled the truck over. 'Are we going to sleep?' I asked. 'Nope, I'm tired,' he answered, and 'you're going to drive. I'll give you a crash course.'" He made sure they were on a smooth, straight highway, showed her how to use the thirteen gears, and crawled into the sleeping berth. She didn't even wake him up to help her maneuver through the one tollbooth on the road. "I realized driving made me pretty happy," says Peach.

One day he asked, "Why don't you go to school and get your truck-driving license?" She started school on her thirtieth wedding anniversary.

"I had the hardest time passing my driving test. My husband called from the road and asked, 'Did you pass your backing-skills test?' I was hysterical, and he said, 'Just stop. I feel bad I got you into this.' Well, that helped me do it."

They started driving together as a team, and the woman who ran the trucking company they worked for called one day and said, "Peach, I've got a trip out to Ohio. Why don't you take it yourself?"

On that first trip alone, Peach got lost for half a day and, not knowing she was two blocks from her destination, sent a message via her truck's satellite to the home office: "I'm locking this truck up and taking the bus home. I can't do it." Her friends back in the office talked her through it, and she got to the destination six hours late. "There was a whole group waiting for me to get there, and they took me out to dinner. It's the worst and nicest memory I have of driving a truck."

Just five feet tall, she's also driven a moving van and packed up whole houses. "I'm pretty strong-willed," she says, "and recently, I took a trip alone to New York City because I knew if I could do that, I could do anything. When I got home, my husband said, 'I am impressed.'

"My son thought I was losing my mind when I started this. He thought I'd come home wearing tight jeans and dangling chains. But my husband has always been supportive. I love driving the truck. I have time to think about things. And although I never would have given up staying home, I really enjoy the freedom I never had."

Claudia and her husband understood as their marriage progressed that one day she would get a chance to pursue her goals. She was a nursery-school teacher when they got married and moved to his New England college town so that he could finish his degree. She never graduated. "But part of having a successful marriage is to realize that you're two people, and you don't have to do everything at the same time," she says.

Their first child was born thirteen months after they got married, right after he graduated from college. Then he started his career in international finance. It was hard for her to have any kind of career if he would be transferred a lot. So she put it on hold.

"I knew that my real job was being with the kids," she says. "I did all the mom things and always talked with my husband about working when the kids were in school. When I wanted to go to work, I realized that I needed to get a college degree. My husband was great. Every day he packed three lunch bags. When he had to travel for his work, my mother was there."

As time went by, she allocated a lot of responsibility to her kids. When they needed something, they got it themselves. "They needed me, to be sure, for emotional crises and home-work," she says. "And for school functions, when I couldn't go, my husband would, or my mother and father. I had a great net-work."

Christine stood by her husband through his desire to prove himself in his family's business and waited until his confidence was high and he was an established leader before she ever thought about going to work.

"I see a lot of women whose husbands are threatened," Christine says, "but my husband always tells his friends and col-leagues how proud he is of me.

"He was brought into his family's successful business, and he wanted to be sure he got whatever he got because of his skills and not his name. If he hadn't gained that confidence in his ability and earned the respect of people in the company, I don't know what would have happened to me, whether I would have gone to work.

"He comes from a strictly traditional family. His mom and sisters don't work, but they do believe that everybody should do something to contribute to the world. They all do civic work and are achievement-oriented. But they were astounded when I went back to work. They never expected it. Today they are pleased and proud of all I have done."

The ultimate support from her husband came for Lynne when they decided to start a computer-consulting business together. She, her husband, and their two children had spent a lot of time together as a family. They loved to take vacations together. Even today, now that they're grown, the children still travel with their parents. In the past few years they've driven to the national parks like Yellowstone and Grand Canyon.

"You think raising your children is your life's work," says Lynne, "but it's such a small part of it. I never understood they would grow up so fast and be gone."

She was always home with the children. And when she wanted a little something else to do, she sold Tupperware. Her family told her they hated that she went out at night, and she quit. "I didn't mind giving it up. But I learned that I had the ability to speak in front of people and sell. It was fascinating to me."

So at the time when her friends started going to work, when their children were teenagers, the women broke up their tennis game, card game, and shopping trips. Her friends became real estate agents, travel agents, and opened boutiques. "I wanted to be in the business world, and I wanted to be with my husband," says Lynne.

It happened at that time that the computer-consulting company he worked for went public, and he lost clout. They started the same kind of business together in their dining room, and Lynne handles the payroll and books. When the salesmen are out on the road, she answers the phones, too, and helps customers with problems.

"It was hard on the kids at first because they had to be quiet when they came home from school," says Lynne. "Then we moved the office down to the basement, and they had to give up their telephone, which is tough for teenagers. I think this has been good for my children. My son has really seen his father in business and knows where he gets his drive and motivation. And my daughter is very confident. When she applied to law school, I asked, 'Why do you want to be a lawyer?'

"She answered, 'Because I don't want to be a doctor.'

"Before we were in business together not many of the customers talked to me when I was with my husband on sales trips because I was a woman. Now they talk to me like I'm an expert because I'm his business partner."

Some husbands, though, will never understand what you're doing.

Marsha went back to work as a social worker when her youngest child was in first grade. "My husband was a very busy attorney, and he didn't take my work very seriously. He felt abandoned, and he didn't help around the house."

She had some help with the children—a succession of ladies from Washington State came to live with them. But it was not easy.

"Once the kids were gone he still felt abandoned. Slowly, he began to understand that women wanted to work as the wives of his colleagues were doing more interesting things. I wasn't home on weekends because I'd often be too busy with work, and he had to turn into a survivor. He wanted to eat, so he had to go to the supermarket. It was quite a thing for him to do. A neighbor saw him pushing his cart and said, 'How the mighty have fallen!' I can laugh about it now, but it was difficult."

You probably have a pretty good sense right now about whether your husband will be your booster when you go back to work. Notice whether he's the kind of man who says, "Don't worry, I did that already," or if you have to thank him profusely every time he takes a dish to the sink or drags the laundry up from the basement. Chances are, you can make some improvement in him, but he won't change entirely.

You do have a spectacular chance of making sure you're raising a son or two who will understand the needs of a wife who wants to go to work. There's all kinds of research these days about protecting, nurturing, and encouraging young girls who seem to lose their personae when they get to be about ten years old. We can help them so that they'll grow up to be productive, fulfilled, happy women.

And now there's research being done about young boys who lose the sweet, caring sides we noticed in them when they were three-year-olds cuddling stuffed animals. People tell them to be tough, fight it out, solve their own problems, and learn to be men without telling them that it's okay to cry, be sensitive, and ask your parents for help. They live by the creed: Boys *must* be boys.

Our boys are going to grow up, have families, and go to

work, too, and if we don't make sure they understand what it means to be caring, loving dads, then they're not going to do all that we wish would come naturally. Let's work on making sure our sons don't think men have to have better jobs, earn more money, and cook fewer dinners than women.

What if your family is not there today weaving a support net for you? Who can you turn to then? You turn to your women friends. That's what Kathy Ruppert did.

Kathy, who is a Ford-dealership service manager, belongs to a crowd its members call Our Group. They're all women between thirty-eight and fifty, who met one another at a swim club. All of them had been home with their kids, who vary in age, but for all of them work became a necessity when they needed the money. One became a medical secretary, one's a dentist's secretary, one went to work for the I.R.S.

"We're all supportive of each other. We listen and compare and share our stress and aggravation," Kathy says. "Because we hadn't been out there working, we weren't sure of how things worked. But we all trust each other and can talk about anything bothering us."

Leila learned after she went back to work that she didn't have much time for socializing anymore, and it bothered her. "I'm bereft and lost without my two closest friends," she says. "I had met them through political volunteer work before I became an attorney. We visit on the phone. I need to remember that I'm a person. And I believe that you always need someone out of your family to blast off to."

After Ellie began her career as an environmental worker, her marriage broke up. She had tried to work doing freelance writing projects for publishers while she was married and raising the children, but her husband kept taking new jobs and the family would move. With the responsibilities of finding new houses and settling her children in new schools taking up her time, it was hard to maintain continuity.

"He always said he was supportive and that my lack of a career was all my fault, but he didn't really want me to be successful. He kept doing things to make sure I didn't progress."

She found her emotional support from her friends and neighbors in the town she lived in near San Francisco. "The kids all played outside in the neighborhood, and the schools encouraged the mothers to get involved. If you go out and get involved, you make wonderful friends. Having women around you who always encourage you and never say you can't do things is a valuable plus in any life."

Whatever your goals are, learn to find strength from those who are on your side.

There are certain things that happen in the working world that will come as naturally to you as carrying enough Kleenex, checking to see if the baby is breathing, and whirling around every time you hear a child say "Mom."

Boys will be boys.

You know how girls are.

Girls like pink. Boys like blue.

Men are rough. Women are soft.

Not exactly the politically correct, gender-equitable thinking of the twilight years of the twentieth century.

We've got a new spin on gender differences lately.

Flipping the dial recently, I saw a commercial for a bank in which a vice president–type man who's obviously in touch with his feminine side says, "You have to be businesslike to meet the challenges *and* remember to have human relationships at the same time. It's really nice when you can balance all that."

Well, yes, it is.

And it's nice that men finally understand the need for balance. With the changing nature of the workplace, with moms and dads alike calling for flexible schedules as well as the ability to work at home and receive equal pay for equal work, this humanistic side of life will be called into play in your job.

Young women are graduating from college now and entering fields that were unheard-of for women years ago. I have a big bound volume of *The New York Times* from 1955, and I was looking at the classified ads to see what kinds of jobs were available then. Maybe you don't remember this, but the Help Wanted sections were divided by gender. Of course, there were pages and pages of Sunday ads looking for able-bodied men to be everything from executives to scientists. Dozens of headings read, "Young Man Wanted." Naturally, there were far fewer positions available for women. The jobs were for secretaries, gal Fridays, advertising copywriters, salesgirls, and assistants of every sort. Some ads even requested an attractive girl.

Segregation according to sex is not so blatant today. Many enlightened companies are realizing that women are an important part of the workforce. What's more, 60 percent of all mothers with children under eighteen go to work, and the business world has concluded that by overlooking women, it forfeits the benefits of bright, well-educated minds that will make their organizations grow.

If you have always thought that men *are* different from women but that those differences don't mean women and men shouldn't be treated as equals, you'll be interested in some of the thoughts circulating these days about the difference between the sexes in the workplace and some of the expectations that employers have of you.

There is a great discourse going on between magazine and book covers and in the halls of business schools comparing the ways in which men and women lead. The experts assess the different traits they believe men and women bring to the workplace. The starting point for the conversation is that women are nurturing, intuitive, collaborative, organized, compromising, compassionate, can think along many lines at once, and are not as power-hungry. Men are said to be less sensitive, more factual, logical, and interested in power.

No matter what else has formed you, shaped you, and influenced you, motherhood, too, has left its print. There's no escaping that you now think a certain way because you have raised children. And maybe this has made you a little more sensitive, intuitive, and adaptable.

Certainly, you've learned a new way to think. I've always

thought that a mother has a peanut-butter-and-jelly attitude toward life and a father has a life-insurance view. That is, the mom is always worried about what is needed in the next three seconds to one week. It's all second nature to her, and she will do anything she has to, from begging a neighbor to watch the children or selling the living room rug to pay for camp tuition. Dad, meanwhile, is often oblivious to these pressing needs, and he gets the opportunity to worry about the long-range concerns such as how the kids are going to go to college and whether they will, indeed, have life insurance.

These skills you develop as a mother become like breathing. You don't even notice that you're such an obvious mom. Even if you never thought it would happen to you, you find yourself comparing brands of apple juice and swapping potty-training stories with other mothers. And you even found yourself so caught up and so enamored of it all that you chose to be home with your children.

When you return to work, you'll find the mom side of your personality to be a great advantage.

The Mom personality caused Heidi to develop a unique reason for wanting to become a mother in the first place. She worked in human resources in a hospital before she had her four children.

"I was inspired by the women I worked with who had children," she says. "They had a far greater grasp of management skills than I did. These women had developed a lot of insight into human nature."

To Heidi, one of the biggest questions in human-resources management was how to motivate an employee. Mothers seemed to have a better grasp of how to find something valuable in a person. They could read a wide variety of nonverbal communication. For them, disciplining an employee was not a matter of punishment but of redirecting their efforts. She was amazed. The mothers would always say, "This stuff works at home."

"If I want to be a better management consultant," Heidi thought, "I should have kids.

"There was some secret here I had to learn," she says. "Every skill I ever learned at work has been tested at home ten times over. My job skills have been enhanced—not lost—by being home with my kids."

What you gain by being at home is an insight into human nature you can't find anywhere else. You can read all the psychology books in the world, but you won't comprehend personality development until you have seen it turn page by page from the beginning.

Cokie Roberts, a national newscaster who covers Congress, shook her head on a Sunday-morning talk show. "I've said time and again that the best preparation for covering Congress is being a mother because they all behave like a bunch of two-year-olds. Look what happened last week. One acted like a two-year-old and got his way. The rest of them see that and think that's the way to get what you want. Ridiculous."

Cokie Roberts didn't have to psychoanalyze these legislators or pontificate like a pundit. She knew exactly what they were up to.

The enlightenment about human nature you receive in your home classroom is invaluable. Georgia runs her own advertising business now. First, she was home in Chicago for ten years with her children. "What happens when you raise kids is that you realize that folks don't start out perfect and won't end up perfect. You, the mother, do the best you can to help your kids be as good as they can be. Mothers really understand the issue of people development. Men don't understand it from the same perspective as a woman, except for the men who are truly involved in parenting."

Marilyn, who's a judge today, went to law school in New York before she was married because she thought she would have to support herself for a while. When she did get married, she kept working as an assistant district attorney. She stopped when she was pregnant with her first child because she had complications that made it necessary for her to be on her back.

She had always intended to stop anyway, because the generation she was from made her want to. Her parents would tell their friends, "We're so proud our daughter is a lawyer. Thank God she doesn't practice." She was extolled for staying home. Also, her husband was adamant that she be home, and it was important for her to please him.

When her children were three, six, and eight, she decided to return to work. "Since I wanted to be very involved with them, I didn't opt for a demanding, high-power practice. I went into practice by myself, then became associated with a firm, but I wasn't on the partnership track."

While her children were growing up, she became active in politics, school, the community. She laid the groundwork over ten years for a new career she wanted as a judge. She was elected a family-law judge.

"Being a mother made me a lot more real in the courtroom. At home I learned a lot about dealing with negative relationships. I had to mediate fights and always keep my cool. That's what you do in court."

A man was testifying one day about what a bad mother his former wife was, how she shouldn't have custody, that she couldn't handle the fights between the kids. Marilyn asked, "What does your ex-wife do?"

"He said, 'She's a school-bus driver.'

"I rolled my eyes. Can you imagine what she handles every day?

"You know, it's a very heady job being a judge. People are so deferential to me. But my kids put me in my place."

Her son came to court when he was thirteen and watched testimony from one of the lawyers in a custody case. The mother was talking about how awful it was when the kids came back from visiting their father because their language was so terrible.

"My son turned to my assistant sitting next to him and said, 'I hope she's not impressed with all this testimony. You should hear *her* language.'"

When her middle child was fifteen, she said, "Mom, how come you always give me such terrible advice?"

"I had to laugh. I said, 'Please don't tell anybody in the courtroom.'"

Applying all that you have learned as a mother can reveal that you learned a lot more at home than you think. Happy Fernandez, the Philadelphia city councilwoman who has three grown sons, says, "Being a mother gave me a lot of firsthand experience I didn't know I was getting. In public meetings when people yell at me irrationally, I remember me as a parent. You have to say, 'No, I won't,' or 'No, I can't,' and 'This is the rule in this house.' Kids love to say, 'I hate you,' and as grown-ups they love to say it to politicians. My style is negotiating, both in the house and in politics."

Doris is a judge who says she draws upon her motherly compassion. She recalled a case in which two opposing lawyers came into her chambers. "The defendant was very ill and probably couldn't stand trial. I listened to these two men argue about whether this person should be forced to appear in court. It was inhuman. I said, 'This defendant must be taken out of jail and transferred to a nursing home to receive the proper care.' That's what they ended up doing. It was the right thing to do, and I don't know why no man had done it before I got involved."

Divorce attorney Harriet Newman Cohen remembers she's a mother all the time. "I find that some of my analytical skills were enhanced by raising children. When you're a mother you have to be able to identify your child's problem before you can help fix it, and you spend all your time helping your children figure out what the problem is. I would say to my children, 'Let's go sit down and talk about what happened.' After we talked, I'd say, 'Do you feel a little bit better?' They would, of course.

"This is exactly how I treat the people who work for me. I handle it in a trusting, intelligent way, not as an adversary. We talk about the crux of the problem, not the fault. I have also learned not to get involved in every single problem at work. Just like at home. There are times when you don't hear, remember, or notice what your children are fighting about. You let them solve it themselves.

"I learned how to handle it all with my children. No matter how busy I am, I can always say yes to new projects. The time seems to expand to the amount of work I take on. I could never tell my children that they couldn't do something because I didn't have the time."

If you go back to work as a teacher, you're *really* going to get a chance to try out those child-rearing skills. Elise says that because she became a middle-school teacher after being home with her four children, "I learned to keep it very simple, to make instructions understandable so the children would succeed. I also let my lesson plans be flexible to allow for the influence of the children. Mothers have to bend all the time. Rigid people don't make good teachers."

She also recalls, "The confidence I had acquired at home enabled me to stand up in front of the class without my knees turning to rubber. I knew what I was doing. I had yelled at my kids for fifteen years.

"When I first went back," she says, "I taught teenagers and tried very hard not to be a mother, just a teacher. I teach college now, and there are older women in my classes. I watch them holding back. They know the answers all the time, but they want to let the children answer. I know how they feel. You always want your own children to have the right answer."

Think about the strongest instinct you have as a mother: protecting your young. Calling that instinct into play will develop your self-confidence to its maximum potential.

That confidence will enable you to stand up for yourself when you're out there in the working world. You carry in your head the knowledge that you've already done something important. You've raised little darlings.

Sandy Freedman found this estimable confidence the first time she ran for mayor of Tampa. "I had some male supporters, and I asked them to help me with fund-raising in the business community. They told me to talk to a big real estate developer in town. He was a Republican, and I am a Democrat, but I was told I needed his support. I knew him slightly because my husband had done some work for him.

"I went up to his big office one day to see him. We sat and talked about the issues. Then he learned forward in his chair and asked, 'How many children do you have?'

"Three."

"How old are they?"

"Seventeen, fourteen, and eleven."

"How do you think you can raise children properly and be a good mother to them if you're the mayor?"

"I glared at him. Then I went into a long, loud, heated diatribe, telling him that these children were already better citizens and had more manners and knew a lot more about government than he did. I picked up my briefcase and stomped out. He did not support me in that campaign, and I won. He later supported me. I knew he never would have asked a man that question. I also know that he would still ask a woman that question today.

"I have told this story hundreds of times to women's groups. I think you know why. When you're a politician, you have to be prepared for anything and always remember what's important. So does a mother."

Nine to five in a glass office building is not everybody's idea of happiness.

There's more than one way to go back to work.

There's full-time, part-time, flextime. There's job sharing, freelance, telecommuting, self-employment, and working at home.

That should make you sigh with relief if you're worried that when you go back you'll never see your child score a field goal, that a mountain of breakfast dishes with oatmeal cemented to them will greet you every evening, that you'll become a slave to traffic reports and be up all night doing laundry.

It's not necessary.

Go back so that you'll *like* what you do. If you've been home, you're used to spontaneity. You've seen the kids perform their little miracles, you've been able to pick up and go to the museum on a Tuesday afternoon, you've been able to meet your husband for lunch and go on vacations. If you give all that up for the five-day work week, you might be miserable.

These days one of the considerations in deciding *what* you want to do is *when* and *how* you want to do it. Once you go to work, you have to honor the commitment you've made to your employer. Decide before your first interview the schedule that you need. Realistically tell yourself how much you have to be available for your family.

When you go into the workforce, you'll see there's a huge amount of bias against women with children. The women who don't have children think you're getting to leave early or getting better hours just because you're a mother, and many men think you should *stay* home with your children.

There's also bias against part-time workers. We live in a society that respects people who spend a lot of time at work. We all talk about how few hours of sleep we need, how busy we are, and how hard we work. But now we're starting to recognize that the quality of work life is important. Part-time work makes many women much happier.

"Many women would go back to work sooner if they could go back on their own terms," says Linda Rush of the advocacy group FEMALE. "Women need flexibility, but this is the real world. We have to change the corporate culture if we want these special arrangements."

The smartest companies realize that their employees work harder when they're happier. Corporations do a lot for their employees these days, from on-site medical facilities, gyms, non-smoking environments, healthy cafeterias, and detox programs.

We women have to let them know that giving us different kinds of schedules will make us better workers. Why should they train a woman for eight or nine years, let her leave to have children, then make it difficult for her to return? If a company can't meet your needs, you have to look for work elsewhere.

If part-time is what you want, you have to negotiate it. There are two steps. First, understand that the two parties involved have to want something to happen before it will. So the employer has to be sold that you are a person of value to the company. After that, you can sell yourself as a part-time worker. Never ask for it first. The employer has to believe it's worthwhile to negotiate. Many employers see giving you part-time work as a favor to you, not them.

Second, you have to remove the objections they have to part-time work. Some employers will tell you that you'll cost more because you'll still want benefits, and they still have to pay overhead. And they don't think they'll get as much work out of you. But of course, most part-timers will tell you they end up working more hours than they're paid for. Find out if there are precedents in that company or in that field. A part-time or flexible schedule is not easy to get, but many women have done it.

Speak up. Up front. After eight years at home with her two sons, Sylvia interviewed for a job as a coordinator for special education in a school system. "In the interview I said candidly that my children come first. I said, 'I need flexibility, otherwise I can't take the job. You want me, take my flexibility.'" With that kind of attitude, she found both the employer and the job she wanted.

You have to ask the right person, a sympathetic person, if you want a custom-tailored schedule. When I returned to work, I wanted to work part-time, too, so I contacted a former boss with whom I'd had a great working relationship and explained my situation. We have a lot of respect for each other, and he listened to me seriously. I explained that I wanted to work a few days a week. Together, we figured out exactly what I could do, and because we had worked together before, he knew that I could deliver on my promises. So we negotiated a salary, and he gave me a desk, a cubicle, and a computer terminal. He explained to the full-time workers in the office that I would have a certain schedule, be available for certain meetings, that I could work on certain projects.

And when I would go into the office, I was able to get to work right away. I knew that my time was limited, so I learned to bypass that thirty minutes it often used to take me to catch up with coworkers and glance at the morning headlines. This is something many returning mothers talk about. We are used to getting a lot done when the kids are at school or watching a video, so we know how to squeeze a lot of work into set-aside time.

If you're still working full-time and want to change your hours, if you haven't had children yet and are wondering how you're going to manage it all, if you can't bear the thought of leaving work entirely and you want to keep your talents pliable, then look for a company that will help you do it.

Where are those employers that understand returning mothers, and how do you find them? The Families and Work Institute in New York City publishes a list of "family-friendly" companies, ones that let both moms and dads be parents. *Working Mother* publishes its annual analysis of the one hundred best companies for moms. Ask your friends. Read the business pages.

This is the kind of thinking you should expect to get from a company that considers itself generous and thoughtful to mothers who want to work creative schedules.

Celia, a lawyer with Rohm & Haas, a chemical company, has two young children. She's worked out a full-time schedule, but she's made it flexible, working a couple of days a week at home. "I always make myself around for the company," she says. "They can always find me. So can my kids. I like to get them to school. If the office calls and asks what's a good time for me to start a meeting, I always tell them nine-thirty. This has worked out perfectly for me. I wanted to be involved with my children's lives, to know their teachers and friends, but I wouldn't be happy if I took my fingers out of work completely."

"All these changes happened by accident," says John Subak, senior manager of the legal department. "When I got to my position, we were filled with a lot of men, and we didn't do well by women lawyers. The legal department was pretty damn weak. I asked a fair number of people to leave, then went out to hire the best and the brightest. I hired several very able lawyers, and many of them were young women.

"Now the issues had to be faced. I didn't want them to leave permanently when they had children. Everyone at the top gave us a lot of freedom. We were able to ignore a lot of traditions. The women in the legal division became the role models for the company, and one of the women in my division heads the equal-opportunities division of the company. In fact, when the Department of Labor came in here to run a glass-ceiling audit, she supervised it."

Subak has children of his own who are entering the workforce. That's what's making many men stand up and take notice of what women want: their daughters and daughters-in-law.

Explaining his program, Subak says, "We decided that we could accommodate less-than-full-time schedules. We started off setting certain criteria for part-time. It had to be readily available to most people, not just for senior people but for secretaries, too."

He established right away that part-time was not compatible with being a manager. Subak told women up front that if they wanted to be managers, they'd have to work full-time. The current view here is that you *can* become a part-time manager, but it's not easy.

The only difficulties the company has run into have been in travel. Some women have adequate child care, so it's not a problem.

"We've tried to be considerate of these concerns. But a woman knows if she can't travel, it will impact her job. I've found that lawyers tend to marry lawyers, so a lot of women have spouses who are very helpful."

It's been a tougher issue for the company with clerks and secretaries who have worked full-time. Now they're starting job sharing, and it appears to be working well. "Our culture here is not that scary, and the managers have open doors," he says. "If you want to negotiate a different kind of schedule, the time is right. It's no longer a closet issue. Confront it. There's such a recognition in corporate America today that a representative sample of talent is women. An employer who's seen as being unaccommodating to women's issues won't be able to hire the bright people the company needs. In any community, the professional women have a pretty good network. They know where to work."

<hr>

I t's also possible to work out a flexible schedule with a company that's not quite so attuned to your needs. Mara is an accountant in the tax department of a top national accounting firm, one that has few women in managerial positions.

Before her son was born, she worked the equivalent of six eight-hour days a week and was well regarded. She was known as a person who would take on big projects from clients and really boost her hours.

When she got pregnant, she went into her boss's office and shut the door.

He looked at her and said, "This isn't good news."

She promised that she was coming back full-time.

Never in the tax department had a woman even come back from maternity leave. When she was on leave, she called the partner in her department and told him that she had hired a baby-sitter. That was important because they really didn't believe that she was coming back. They tested her and gave her a project to do during maternity leave.

"I was going stir-crazy on maternity leave," she recalls. "I couldn't wait to go back to work. I worked ten months full-time. It was easy when my son was an infant. He didn't care that I went to work. Then I started having more fun with him. I saw the handwriting on the wall. I wanted part-time."

She talked to a friend in the firm's New York office who had been at a seminar at which the working mothers had gotten together to talk among themselves about how they had worked out their scheduling needs. Her friend suggested she talk to the human-resources director, a woman. She was very helpful. "There's no policy on anything," she told her. "Ask for everything you want."

Mara wrote up a memo for her bosses describing in detail how she would work and the key tasks that she would do in her job. Fulfilling these tasks would be the basis for her evaluations, which furnish the criteria for her bonuses, raises, and promotions. She used flextime terminology in this memo.

"It was very official. I wanted it to be perfect, all spelled out. My bosses didn't seem to see the importance of having all this in writing. They've never signed the agreement, nor has it been finalized. But I don't work five days a week. I got what I wanted."

The women in her department see her as a hero, and women from all over the firm, even out-of-town offices, tell her first when they get pregnant and seek her advice.

"This is a good profession for part-time. You can always pick up books, learn the regulations. Any woman who wants flexibility has to ask others how they did it. Then make a plan. Know what you want."

For some women the ideal working life is exactly twenty hours, two and a half days per week. The lucky ones are able to work it out. Margie is one of them.

She is a lawyer who works for a large metropolitan transit agency, after having practiced for ten years as an associate at big firms before she had her first child.

"I knew that I was going back to work in some capacity," Margie says, "because I had a vested interest in it. I couldn't, though, go back to a big firm. It's not the kind of thing you want to do if you want to have a family. I billed a minimum of eighty hours a week. Working until eight at night was a normal day. When the big crunches came, I'd be there forever."

She heard about a job in the legal department at the agency and was immediately attracted to the hours: from eight-thirty until four-thirty. When she started working there, she was shocked to see people actually leave at four-thirty.

"You never dare leave a big firm early. I could take my daughter to a play group in the afternoon! On play-group day I wouldn't take lunch and would leave at three-thirty. Nobody blinked!"

After a year there, she got pregnant again. She really wanted a second child but knew there was no way she could split her time between two children and a job. A man she knew at a big firm told her she could come work there part-time as other mothers were doing. "But I knew that part-time there meant forty hours a week."

She went to her supervisor, a woman, and said that she would have to leave because she wanted to look for a part-time job. The supervisor said, "This is an idea whose time has come. Figure out how to split your position in the middle, and we'll support you." This had never been done here before.

Margie found another woman with a young child. Essentially, they became partners, and they share all the cases that come up.

They agreed each would work two-and-a-half days and that they'd overlap for lunch on Wednesday to talk about what was going on.

Margie made it clear to her employers that she would not need to use their health benefits because she could be on her husband's plan.

"Still, they took away all my sick time, all vacation time, and all my pension," she said. Plus they could pay me less! Nevertheless, my partner and I were so thankful! And our employer was in seventh heaven. If my partner or I have to be out, good little girls that we are, we always cover for each other."

Over the years they have tried to get back some of what they lost. Margie got her sick days back and disability.

And the two women have become good friends. They've brought their children to the office, and the kids have picnics under the desk.

"I had the big-firm thing and chose to leave," Margie says. "This is better. I have a different kind of confidence and attitude here. I can ask for what I want, even a court date to be changed, without thinking I am jeopardizing my whole career. That's not the big-firm way of life."

Eventually, Margie and her partner, Jan, would like to go full-time, once their children are older. "Our dream is to manage the litigation department. I don't know how we'll ever get it. But we're also talking about opening a little shop together. Who knows?"

B ut if you think that going back into an office at all isn't right for you, then consider working at home and keeping your office contacts to a minimum. A great advantage to working at home is that you can keep your own hours, whether you want to work early in the morning or very late at night.

One of the waves of the future is telecommuting along the fiber-optic network. If you know how to work on a personal computer, you're in great shape. If you don't, you have to learn, because before you can say *gigabyte*, your livelihood will depend on it.

Telecommuting means you're in contact with your employer via computer modem, floppy disks, phone, and fax. It's great. I've had freelance jobs in which I fax copy back and forth for a day, then send my floppy disk to the client when they're ready to set type. It gives you a lot of freedom. For those moms who are looking for a whole new way to work, you'd be best served to talk to a small business that would like your talents but doesn't want to pay your overhead. And if you already have your own computer, they'd be most interested to hear from you.

The working-at-home thing is terrific because you can go to school plays without asking anybody's permission and schedule your meetings in accordance with *your* schedule. You don't have to have a huge wardrobe of office clothes, and you don't have to commute.

The biggest drawback is that many people will think that you don't work. I find that nobody knows what a writer does anyway, and nobody ever really sees me work, so many people think I'm available to volunteer for everything. Maybe it's just a problem for women. I saw a television interview with a male author who used to have a "real" job, as he put it, in an office. When he quit the job and started writing, he told the interviewer, he felt so free, so unencumbered, as if he were not working. He would tell his friends why he felt so happy, and they'd say, "That's silly. Of course you work. You're a writer." Uh-uh. This isn't how it works with me.

You also need to make your family aware of your job's responsibilities.

Hire a baby-sitter to busy your children while you're working. Make a lunch date with the kids so you can catch up during the day. They do know you're at home, after all. And when they're older, make them understand that when you're on a business call, it means you can't be interrupted.

"My husband taught me that you have to set limits," says Eleanor, who runs an author-escort business from her home. "When he left his job and started a consulting business at home, I asked him to help with a lot of my errands. He said, 'I cannot drive the car pool or do the grocery shopping. I'm trying to start a business here.' Women have to do this."

We sure do, but it's hard. Says Francesca, who runs a marketing-consultant business from her Dallas home, "I'm busy all day, but my husband still comes home and says, 'What did you make for dinner?' and doesn't do any chores around the house. He used to help cook and shop before we had children and both worked in offices, but now he thinks I'm home all day, so I should do everything. It seems to him that because he's out he must be working harder."

It is difficult to be disciplined and take yourself seriously when you're working at home. You know how it is. You're ready to do that work, but you can see into the open closet, and it looks like such a mess that you know you'll feel anxious all day if you don't clean it out. You'd never be like that if you went to an office. But you have to learn to give your work work precedence over your mom work, especially after you've just spent all that time doing mom work alone.

One help is to have a space that's devoted to your outside work. It doesn't matter how fancy. Laurie discovered this early when she started a home business. First it was in a closet, into which she stuffed a desk. She kept the door closed when she was working, and the children knew not to rap on the door or ask any questions.

"I could hear them whispering out in the hall, 'Do you think she's in the closet?' Then I moved to the dining room, then to the den, where I am now. Every time I moved, it was because I took my business more seriously, and it was growing."

Even though you might have to work around a lot of obstacles (men are banging new gutters onto my home as I write this), there are ways to do it.

Forget those ads that say you'll make six figures a year selling magazine subscriptions or addressing envelopes. You don't care about selling something that means nothing to you. Do you have a hobby? Are you good at something? Use your own talents. If you can bake, cook, knit, sew, draw, paint, decorate, cut hair, grow flowers and vegetables, sing, write, take photographs, or make party favors, turn it into a business.

Start a newsletter about one of your interests. Teach other moms to do what you do. Get certified by a software company to give computer lessons. Sell toys, cookware, crafts, cosmetics, or clothing made by companies you believe in. Plan weddings, parties, and meetings for people who don't have the time or inclination. Help people fill out their medical-insurance forms. Start a service to help people find contractors, plumbers, roofers, electricians. If it's too overwhelming to do alone, start it up with a friend. You'll have someone to share your anxieties with, someone who will take your late-night calls.

Go to a local community college or university or call your chamber of commerce and find out about small-business startups. There's information for you about business plans, loans, legalities, even special bonuses just for women.

Look at all those women who are on television with home-improvement shows that feature other women who have started businesses making draperies, baskets, napkin rings, closet organizers, place-card holders, and dried-flower wreaths. Don't you think they were probably moms at home not too long ago? Now they work from home and feel terrific about themselves.

You'll be welcomed eagerly to the World of Guilty Working Mothers.

By the time you get to fourth grade, somebody in your class has visited Yellowstone National Park and reported on the big thermal pools filled with scalding, dusky-colored waters that bubble up along the surface. They sound really scary. As you walk the imagined treacherous path among these huge, angry puddles, any second you could stumble, fall in, and boil away to nothing.

Pleasant.

This is pretty much how a working mother feels.

Not only does she walk this path of looming dangers and natural disasters every day, but she believes that she actually *deserves* to tumble in.

OUACHITA TECHNICAL COLLEGE

Everybody, from her mother to her male boss to parenting magazines to politicians to her sister-in-law who chose to be home with the children, makes her feel horrible.

She, they remind her, is not the perfect mother. The perfect mother is one who is home, who is present for every milestone, every play date, and every trip to the emergency room.

The working mother is the guilty party.

You, however, who have stayed home, are perfect.

And now you want to do what she does.

Ah, well.

Fear not, because when you go back to work, you'll join a coterie of women who stand together and worry that their working has caused them to wreak havoc on their significant others and children. You can't help it. Worrying about children is a mother's encumbrance. The other working mothers just help you lift it onto your shoulders every morning.

Content yourself with the notion that you've made a choice that has comforted you. You've been home with your children while they were small. Now keep in your mind that you're going to be comfortable again, that when you get that eruption of new self-esteem, any guilt you're about to feel cannot possibly devastate you.

Donna Lieberman, an attorney with the A.C.L.U. in New York, is a mother of two who thought she had it all figured out before her first child was born. Guilt never entered her plans. In fact, her mother had worked while she was growing up and still regretted having to miss Donna's school play in kindergarten. Donna would make sure she'd never repeat that.

But over the years, after she went back to work, she discovered that the guilt happens as sure as the children grow up.

She became pregnant when she directed the Association of Legal Aid Attorneys in New York and planned to work right up until the baby was born. But she hurt her back, couldn't stand up, and went from her bed to the chiropractor.

In the meantime, she had planned to take a year off to be with the baby.

During that year she found a friend she had lost touch with and realized that having the companionship of women was important. Other friends with babies told her she had to line up a regular baby-sitter so that she could get out. She rediscovered making pottery and met her friend for lunch. It was an easy, comfortable time.

"Being home with my son made me feel pretty mellow," she recalls. "It gave me time to breathe and the opportunity to think about what I was going to do next. I knew that when I went back to work I would take a job I liked and felt comfortable doing because I understood that having kids is an extension of the things you do with your life."

Her first child was small when she returned to work, and she felt pangs leaving him, but she knew they'd manage. "It's far more onerous now that they're eight and twelve not to be home," Donna says. "When they were younger all they needed was a warm, stimulating person who could change their diapers and play with them. I worry that as they get older and have more freedom that it wouldn't hurt to have parental help.

"The kids and I both suffer," she says. She comes home from work at seven, and instead of having the patience to ask questions about their days, she cuts right to the jugular. When you work all day, it's harder to feel up to the challenge of the kids at night. She worries now more than ever about what's going on with them.

"My work is important," says Donna, "but nothing can hold a candle to the responsibility I have in my kids' lives. I drop whatever I'm doing when one is sick. I try not to compromise the needs of my kids." Still it happens.

Moms may feel in control, but kids have the real power over us. They can bring us to our knees with a whine, a pout, a tantrum. And their criticism can cut into our motherly hearts.

You think you're doing the right thing by staying home. But what do they think?

Hannah found out. Her family needed more money coming in, but she was determined to be home with the children while they were small. A part-time job in a department store working half days when her daughter was in nursery school seemed just right. "I loved helping people pick china," she says. "But every morning my daughter was throwing tantrums, and I felt so guilty that I quit. I told my daughter about this when she was twenty-four. 'That was dumb!' she said. 'I would have gotten over it.'"

Adair, who went to work as a chef, remembers how jealous her children felt when she didn't cook for them anymore. "My children were jealous because I was so happy," she says. "The worst part for them was when I started working three days a week. I'd stick some stuff in a Crock-Pot in the morning for their dinner. My fourth child said, 'Just don't ever forget that the Crock-Pot is the symbol of the awfulness of your working.' Even if the food had been divine, she would have complained."

Gretchen is a financial consultant in New York who went back to work when her children were twelve, eight, and six. "I was around when they were small, and I felt good about that," she says. "The one thing I regretted was not being home between three in the afternoon and eight at night. They have so much to share then. If you're not there after school, they've forgotten about it by the time you come home. My kids would look at me angrily, go to their rooms, and have nothing to say to me."

Sometimes it seems it's the duty of young children to make their mothers feel guilty if they don't think of them every single minute or don't behave the way children think mothers should.

But that resentment is going to happen whether you're home all day or not. Your going off to work is not in itself going to have a negative effect. It's far worse to be at home and feel depressed, stifled, embittered, and without choices or emotional support than to go to work and make your life better.

Don't make your children your excuse for not finding work if you want it. Your children are a lot more resilient than you might think.

Shelley started her own crafts business, which demanded a lot of her time, and she still kept up all of her mom responsibilities. If one of the kids left a lunch box at home in the morning, she'd have it at school by noon. She decided she was being crazy. "'Look, troops,' I told them, 'I will do anything in the world for you the night before, but you have to be responsible for yourselves when I'm working.'"

Now she says it helped her children. They became more independent and realized they had to do chores around the house. The truth is you can't be with your children twenty-four hours a day anyway, whether you're a mom at home or at work.

Helen Cooke chose to return to social work when her son was ten. She thought he was ready, but she remembers his being disappointed when she wasn't eligible for a vacation day to attend a luncheon at school to which the parents were invited. "Of course, he was the only one without a parent, and he came home at the end of the day and told me he had eaten all by himself. It was a sad thing to picture, but I had to focus on something positive. I congratulated him. Then I told him that we're disappointed in life sometimes but I would make sure we would do other things together. He got over it quickly."

The kids really love you, and they can benefit from your working.

Ann, a nurse, says, "Children can really humble you. They put you through a whole gamut of emotions. Dealing with it made me a lot stronger. I wasn't afraid to be humbled."

When she went to nursing school, it was good for her kids. They started competing with her and checking her tests to see how she was doing, to see if it was worth it for her to be in school. "They resented that there was so much attention on me after all these years I had done nothing but be their mom. They were used to my husband and me praising *them* for their schoolwork. One of my sons hadn't been doing so well in school, but after I started going, his grades picked up right away.

"He was pretty quiet about his feelings. But one day I looked through his school bag and found a paper he wrote. It was about me, saying he felt so good about what I did."

Working mothers can chew themselves up with guilt. And outsiders feel free to take advantage of it.

My husband came home one day and tossed *The Wall Street Journal* of July 23, 1993, on the table. "Here's a story that will drive you nuts," he said.

The main headline of this front-page story read, "Stay-at-Home Moms Are Fashionable Again in Many Communities." One subhead declared, "Former Professional Women Bring Competitive Edge to Bake Sales, the PTA." And another asked, "Are Their Kids Better Off?"

Declaring that a wife at home was comparable in status to a BMW in the driveway, the story claimed that full-time motherhood had become "downright chic." It quoted a dad saying, "It's not something you brag about, but it's a source of pride."

The story went on to say there is "universal agreement among women that their children turn out better than those of mothers who work outside the home." One mother was quoted referring to day-care centers as "those little meat factories." Another mother said of a neighbor boy who threw rocks at a squirrel, "That little boy's mother works, but I can be around to reinforce values."

The Wall Street Journal was confused about the reasons that women go to work. We're not taking jobs and cobbling careers so that we can impress our husbands and their colleagues. We're working to help support our families and make ourselves feel better. And that's just fine.

Thinking that some mothers are better than others fuels the mommy wars, which have been stoked and nourished by people who want to create divisions between mothers. There's no reason to pit mothers who love their children against other mothers who love their children. It's harmful, and it tells *our* children that they're not free to pursue the kinds of lives that will make them happiest.

It is so confusing to go to work. You don't know what to think of yourself. One day you're doing the right thing. One day you're doing the wrong thing. You don't know who you identify with anymore.

Sue worked as a speech pathologist in St. Louis, then stayed home with her children until she start helping her husband in his business. When she had a career, she looked down on moms at home. When she had children, she thought she should stay home. "It seemed like the right thing to do, but I was bored, and I felt guilty. When people asked me what I did, I would say, 'I'm working at being home with my children.'"

Now that she's working again, she feels guilty that she's not with her kids.

"And I'm so much more exhausted," she says. "I think you have to use more energy when you're out in the world. The children are physically tiring, but the mental and physical combination is stressing me out. When I get stressed out, it shows in our family life."

What is our society doing to moms like her?

When Samantha returned to work as a stockbroker, she observed, "Everyone seemed to have a narrow, middle-class view that I ought to be at home instead of out earning a living. Even our pediatrician was dreadful. He told me that my kids would end up in the gutter. I looked around his office, and all I saw were working mothers—the nurses."

Many women who go back to work feel guilty on the job, and it becomes an overriding concern for them. When you've devoted all that time—so many years—to being with your family, it's going to be a huge worry when you go to work. How much are you taking away from them? You have to stop and look at what's being demanded of workers now. People are being asked to work harder and longer because there are so many cutbacks. Companies are asking those who are left to do more.

This leads to a lot of stress. You're worried about your family, and you're worried about keeping your job. Then, of course, you have to remember that you need time for yourself. This stress could get very unhealthy.

You have to make sure your employer has reasonable expectations of you. It's important to be assertive about what you will and won't do. Because just as you have taken on all these tasks in the house, you'll end up taking on everything at work. *Women take it more.*

When you go back, you're trying to prove yourself in everything. Many women feel they have to be the last one to go home at the end of the day or do all these tasks that are not in their job description and that no one has even asked them to do. If you feel you can't ever leave the company, that no one else would ever hire you, you allow yourself to be abused. They'll take advantage of you. And you probably won't even ask for more money. What's more, you get bogged down in your job and stop networking and keeping yourself marketable.

A mother who goes to work is giving her children a great deal. The most important part of raising children is making them understand that no matter what job you do, you care for them more than anything in the world. That's where they get their self-esteem and confidence. And by seeing you pursue your dreams, work hard, and reap rewards, they'll have a solid, assured role model they can emulate.

You don't have to feel guilty.

You have to do what's necessary for your family.

And someday your child might talk about you the way Thea talks about her mother.

Thea is a woman in her thirties who produces a National Public Broadcasting series for teenagers. Her mother made tremendous sacrifices while her four daughters were growing up. But she knew that's what she had to do to support the children. She also taught her kids a valuable lesson.

Her mother was born and raised in a small town in Ohio. She left when she was seventeen to go to college, then move to New York. She became a secretary, joined the Navy, and met her husband at a Navy fair forty years ago.

They moved to San Diego, where her mother went to work in motion pictures as secretary first to Burt Lancaster, then Tony Curtis, then Ray Bradbury. She stopped working to have her four girls in three years and ten months. Thea has a twin sister.

At a very young age, Thea was diagnosed with minimal cerebral palsy on her left side.

"My mother was determined to make me strong," Thea says. "Before I was diagnosed, my mother always picked me up when I would cry and scream after falling. On the day she found out I had cerebral palsy, at eighteen months, she didn't pick me up again. She would let me sit out in the yard for an hour until I figured out how to get into the house."

With four children it became clear to her parents that they couldn't cut it on one income. Her mother knew she had to go to work, but was adamant that she be home during the day for her kids. She still wanted to go on the school trips, pack them special lunches, and be home at the end of the school day. So she took a job as a clerk steno at the Los Angeles Police Department and worked from midnight to seven-thirty in the morning for ten years. It was just ten minutes from their house, so she was home by the time the girls got up in the morning and could help them with their hair, then help Thea to the car in her wheelchair.

"Of course we knew she was always tired," recalls Thea.

"When kids would kick my wheelchair or call me Robot Leg, she'd tell me, 'These kids are afraid of the unknown. Rise above them. They want to rattle you.'

"Today I'm not in a wheelchair anymore, but I tripped walking this afternoon, and some teenage boys laughed at me. I said to them, 'If I can provide a little laughter in your day, then my fall made it all worthwhile.' This was my mother talking."

When Thea first went to work in television production, the only job she could get was on an overnight shift. "If my mother could do it, so could I," she says. "My mother had always gotten dressed up for work even though she worked overnight. So did I."

"I was very nervous when I started in news. She said, 'Don't get upset. If you're afraid of trying, then you have a problem.' I would not be a producer of a national television show now without my mom."

Thea's mother is now retired. Recently she's started rock climbing. "I said that I wanted to do it, too, with her and my husband," says Thea. "My dad said, 'Don't let her do it.' But my mom answered, 'If she wants to, let her.' She stood at the bottom giving me silent encouragement by watching me. She didn't say, 'Come on, Thea, you can do it.' She just watched. I did it. I got to the top. And I gave her a big hug. I don't look at my life as anything but blessed."

It won't be long before words like *nanoseconds, quality initiatives, networking, databases,* and *macroeconomics* are tripping off your tongue.

If any of these words sound like a foreign language to you, you've been out of the workforce a long time, dear.

There are a lot of ways to find out what's going on in that world that's continued to whirl as you've entered your own homespun orbit. Babies have started on rice cereal for decades, but the work world hasn't stopped for a second.

Or a nanosecond. Those semiconductors make information run pretty fast these days.

You may be out of work right now, but if you're thinking of going back, you have to know how to get there.

The first way is through networking.

These days over 80 percent of all jobs are found through people you know. Everybody you know is part of your network. And the way to network is to talk to them. Tell anybody who could be helpful to you that you want to go back to work. Have your husband tell his friends. Let your mother ask her friends. Tell your reading group, your neighbors, your car pool. You never know where your first paycheck will be coming from.

If you want to go back into your old, premom business, get in touch with people you used to work with. Call your old contacts and suppliers. Somewhere you'll hear some bit of information that could become a floodgate of names and ideas. Plus, many of your former colleagues have probably moved on to new companies—or started their own. Find them, and find out what they're doing.

All this is exactly why you should never burn your bridges at your old job.

Whenever I've needed to find new work, when a freelance source has dried up or moved on, I've gotten on the phone and called people who might know of some new person I can call. I keep my eyes on the business pages. And I never say no. I call everybody, meet with everybody whose name I'm given. I always send follow-up letters along with a business card. (Have cards and stationery done at a local quick-printing place. You'll look and feel more professional. Plus, everybody always trades cards. It's worth the cost, and it's tax-deductible.)

The National Association for Female Executives (NAFE) publishes a booklet, "Networking Know-How," which gives you twenty-one tips for building and maintaining career contacts. Yes, yes, these are written for women who are already in the workforce, but many of the same procedures can work for you. For instance, NAFE encourages you to set goals of people you want to call, plan a strategy for how to call, set yourself a timetable, seek every opportunity to meet new people, then practice network etiquette like following through on promises you make to send along articles or phone numbers. And, most important, NAFE reminds you to push yourself. This isn't easy!

Networking looks like a challenge that can be met only by expert backslappers or by women who just *love* to go to parties where they don't know a soul. Not necessarily. You're not trying to get a date, you're trying to get a job. You have a specific purpose in talking to all these new people. Keeping that in mind, along with your need to foot the college tuition, which is supposedly doubling in the next ten years, will enable you to call people.

Barbara Greenberg, who helps run the nontraditional-student program at Chatham College, discovered the benefits of networking when she wanted to return to the workforce after raising her kids.

"I used to go to my son's Little League games in jeans," Barbara says, "and there was always one mother there who was dressed in a suit. Since I was thinking about going back to work and was interested to know how she combined motherhood and a career, one day I went up to her and asked what she did. She told me she was an admissions counselor for a career school that taught technological job-training skills.

"She had empathy for what I was feeling. So she suggested that we have lunch to talk about how I could do something. At lunch I told her that I had been involved in career testing and job placement. We agreed that her school would be a perfect place for me to work. It was in my field, I could be home at three o'clock for my kids, and I wanted the summers off."

Barbara went to the school without an appointment because she didn't want to send a resume with an unexplained time gap on it. "I knew I had to knock on the door and sell myself. I became friendly with the receptionist, another tip that I recommend. I told her that I had met the woman who is the head of admissions and that she suggested I see Mr. So-and-So. Because we had chatted and gotten friendly, the receptionist called him, said I was there, and I got in to talk to him right then. I was there for two hours, and he offered me a job.

"This is the best of networking. I don't believe in answering newspaper ads. Rarely does a mature woman get a job through the paper."

Women are very successful at networking. They're open and ready to talk and help one another. Barbara had worked with men in their thirties and forties who had been laid off from steel mills. They wouldn't talk about it.

"If you don't talk about it and don't let people know you need some help, you won't know what's out there for you," she says. "I taught these men how to network and showed them how to take their skills and transfer them to other fields. People want to hire those who really want jobs and are creative about finding them."

It's not so hard to find out where the jobs are. The library is full of information. Look up industries and jobs that relate to your interests and your college major. When you drop off your children for story hour, let the librarian entertain them while you read magazines and write down the names of companies and people to contact. There are lots of books and consultants who can tell you how to dress, how to interview. Use all of this stuff. Build your contacts.

Many, many women think they're returning to work just to find a job that will fill their days and their bank accounts. They don't want to become too mentally immersed in their work because that's what made them think working and mothering was a bad combination in the first place. And they often don't have the confidence to think that they could have an honest-to-goodness career.

But when you've devoted the kind of energy to your kids that you have, when you've made sure that they are wonderful, and when you realize that you now need another outside interest to round out your experiences, you'll find you want to get your mind involved as well.

Many returning mothers whom you look at admiringly now never thought they were going to have careers. It's not what they were looking for. But they came to the conclusion that feeling dissatisfied at work, not committed to a goal, made them feel empty. Part of being successful at work is letting yourself learn about things like quality initiatives, accepting and acknowledging that you'll work a lot more efficiently if you use a computer. It's not cute or charming to not understand. It just cuts you off from developing in your job.

Most of all, know that it's okay to like going to work.

So believe that you can be a success.

Set goals for yourself.

And congratulate yourself when you reach them.

You can't imagine, sitting at home now, what can happen to you when you go to work.

Kathy Ruppert was not going to work to run the world. Her entry into the workforce was dictated by the need for money, just like many of us. She'd been home for fourteen years raising her two children and getting dinner on the table at four-thirty every afternoon when her husband came home from work.

"I was involved with everything my children did," says Kathy. "That was my career, my fulfillment." When she and her husband faced bills for braces and the rising costs of sending their children to Catholic school, she turned to the classified ads.

While the children were in school, her work experience had been part-time, helping in a friend's catering business and cleaning houses, but she wanted something more interesting. A clerk's position at a Ford dealership caught her eye. It was close to home, and the ad didn't ask for any experience. She went in and met the owner, who took an instant liking to her and hired her on the spot as assistant to the manager who ran the department that preps new cars and reconditions trade-ins.

"I was really like a secretary," says Kathy, "but it's my nature to get in there and learn how everything works. I work this hard with everything, ever since I had polio as a kid. I have to be self-sufficient."

Soon after she started, her boss had to have a liver transplant and was out for two months. Fortunately, she had paid attention. They didn't hire anyone to replace him while he was gone, and Kathy really ran everything. When he came back, he wasn't well enough to work, and they let him go. The owner came to Kathy and said, "We want you to run it. You've done a good job." She started out running the reconditioning department, and the job kept ballooning. They asked her to do new-car preps, too.

"Having a job is a lot of responsibility and a lot harder than I ever thought," she says. "This job is very time-consuming. I'm not able to leave it. It goes home with me, and I wake up at three A.M. thinking I forgot this or that. My boss tells me that I give one hundred fifty percent.

She has to work that hard to make it in her job because the service division of a car dealership is traditionally a man's world. You can imagine the funny looks this petite, feminine, well-dressed woman with carefully styled red hair gets back in those service bays. "The best way to handle these men comes from being a mother," she says. "First of all, we're talking about a lot of car mechanics who aren't used to having women around at work. I didn't like their language. I said to them, 'You're going to watch your mouth in front of me. I don't have people talk to me or in front of me like that.' It worked. I always try to maintain my femininity."

Her boss tells her, "You're a mother hen to those boys. They always tell you their personal problems. Be a manager."

"Well, I think I am," she says, "but I don't yell at them. Instead, I embarrass them. If they don't sweep up the service bay, I go out and do it. It worked with my kids. I can handle these guys a lot softer than the male bosses."

And she finds that she can draw on her experiences as a mother to help her. She learned that her first firing was going to be a father of two babies right at Christmas. It took her two days to be able to call him in. "I cried and apologized. I begged, borrowed, and stole to get him a new job the same day. I do that a lot. I know these guys are family men."

And when women came into the dealership with car problems, she always felt that she was listening to her kids, trying to identify what was wrong and help fix it. So she started women's nights for women in the community to come in and take classes on what to look for in the engine, how to check the oil and transmission fluid.

What's next? "Ford has never had a female service manager, and I'd like to be the first one in the world. Service manager is a big, big job. I feel I can tackle it, but I'm scared. I want to keep on moving higher and higher.

"I'm not amazed at what's happened to me, but I never thought my life would be like this. I'd like to know now what you do after you reach a certain goal, and you have a new one. I'm working on it myself now."

Another field where women are whacking through the gender kudzu is politics. When you were growing up, did you ever imagine all these women elected officials? There were some women involved, but they all seemed to be of a certain age and to have inherited their offices from their husbands. These days politics is not only more receptive to women, it's actually tenable for somebody like you. You won't exactly be chosen as the presidential candidate your first time out, but you can enter on a comfortable local level surrounded by your friends and supporters.

Sandy Freedman, the mayor of Tampa, was a mom at home like you.

She had been volunteering in local politics for years, and when a seat became available on Tampa's city council, she decided to run for it. She was in a very tight race of at least seven candidates, and she was feeling discouraged because she couldn't get that all-important newspaper endorsement. So one morning when she was supposed to be appearing at a farmers' market at 5:00 A.M. and saw torrential rains out her window when the alarm went off at four, she turned to her husband and said, "I'm not going to that damn market in this rain." He said, "Get out of bed. You've gone this far and worked this hard." So she went, dripped through the market in the rain, and won the race.

"I learned right then that the voters want to see the candidate," she says. "It takes tremendous effort to do this."

She served on city council for twelve years and was its first woman chair. Although it was supposed to be a part-time job, it turned into a forty-hour work week for her. Now she's been mayor of Tampa for more than seven years.

"I like being in politics on the local level," she says. "You can make something happen. The mayor really runs this city, so I have a lot of responsibility. I love it."

Many women tell her they want to get into politics and ask how to do it. "The first thing to do," she says, "is volunteer and get knowledgeable. Work for a woman candidate and see what she has to do. If you want to run for office, pick some issues that are important to you and become associated with them. Of course, there are different rules for women politicians. Women have to be better informed, better prepared, and look better. You're expected to get dressed up every day. And you don't get to spend much time with your friends."

She decided once that she needed to run a very professional mayoral campaign, and hired one of those big-time political consultants. "He gave me all kinds of rules he had used with women candidates. You can't wear a lot of jewelry or sling-back shoes or open-toe shoes or risqué fabrics like silk, which smack of being rich. Hair and makeup must be done. Don't carry a pocketbook when you debate a male candidate. Only wear pants when a man needs to have your message in his face."

It's also interesting that for a long time she never smiled in public. In fact, many people didn't think she ever smiled. She thought that as a woman in politics she had to be so intense and take herself so seriously. "I've worked hard on that," she says. Of course, if you smile too much, the people think you're just having fun."

Sometimes figuring out where you can be successful is like looking for your car keys. They're always in the last place you look. And right in front of your face.

That's what happened with Ann Gaither. She wanted to go back to work, but she never wanted to go into her family business. A tire-distribution company? A woman?

"If you're an achiever and sitting at home with children," says Ann, "you do everything with a vengeance. I was a rabid volunteer. I needed something to occupy my mind while I was doing all the mundane stuff. I'm not one of those people who enjoys being home. I didn't want to do it forever. I'd been a teacher before my children were born. I was itching to get out of the house."

Her youngest was four and her oldest was fourteen twenty-five years ago when she figured out something to do. Her husband was in his family's hosiery-manufacturing business in North Carolina. "At that time all women's hosiery buyers were men. 'Men can't even talk about this product,' I told my husband. 'Why don't I go out on the road to sell? I'll be the expert of the day.'"

It was a good idea, but it required that she travel a lot, and she didn't want to leave her children. But that brief experience made her realize that she wanted to be in business.

Around that time her father, who ran her family's tire business, became very sick. He asked Ann and her husband to go to New Orleans to a convention in his place.

"He wanted my husband to take over the business. My husband was automatically taken to all the conferences, while I was sent to the teas, tours of homes, and bridge parties with the other wives. I sat in that hotel room fuming while he was at meetings. It was *my* family business, and he didn't know a damn thing about it. The only reason he was going to run it is that he's got a penis."

She told her husband that she was going to learn the tire business, and that was okay with him. He didn't even want to do it. Then she told her father, who welcomed her.

"It was a great relief to me. I had explored going into business with friends, all the different things women look at, but family was not anything I'd thought of. For women it's terrific. You get a chance without having to prove yourself to get your foot in the door. My mother has never understood why I do the things I do, and she thought I was crazy." Now she's grateful because Ann's father got much sicker, and Ann was the only family member in the business. They wouldn't have a business now if Ann hadn't been there.

"One of the blessings was getting to know my father as an adult. He saw my ambition and how my mind works. I got to see the respect that people have for him. I gave him continuance. He lived fifteen years while I was in the business. He got to see what would happen to his company."

When she first started, one executive vice president didn't like her being there. He had a desk in her father's office, and when she joined the company, he asked for his own office. He thought the worst thing he could do for Ann was to make her share an office with her father.

"Of course, it turned out to be the best," she says. "I sat in with my father, and I was privy to every bit of information that came in there. Every time he headed down the hall for a meeting, I'd say, 'Can I go along?' I learned very early how to choose your battleground. Not every one is worth fighting."

Originally, she had come to get out of the house, not to run a company. But when she began to love it for the sense of accomplishment it gave her, she knew it was her career. It was more than a job that passed the time. "If you don't love your work," she says, "you have a job. With a job, you get more personal time, make less money, and control your destiny less. With a career, you'll reap more rewards. But you get the credit and the blame for everything, too.

"This all came at the right time for me," observes Ann. "Once you're past your thirties, you know who you are. You've had to examine your values and pass them on to your kids. You've answered the tough questions. And things you did when you were twenty no longer appeal to you. I was ready."

Ann speaks to a lot of working women, and after one speech a woman asked what she considered the most important things for a woman to know.

"I told her that first, I wished every woman had my father. But the most important thing for women to have is confidence to listen to ourselves. We always look to others for the answers. But we have it inside of us."

She recalls sitting in a meeting and coming up with a thought. She said it, and no one paid any attention. A few minutes later, a man said something close to it, and the rest of the men thought he was brilliant. "I thought to myself, 'I've had better thoughts than that but never had the confidence to say them out loud.'"

It was a turning point for Ann, one that made her understand that she really knew the business and was willing to take responsibility for it. She knew she was ready to put herself on the line. As she says, "I learned to be a risk taker. The more you take, the more confidence you get. And nobody ignores you."

Your career path can look as clear as a Rorschach inkblot.

Back in the *Leave It to Beaver* days, moms went home after giving birth and stayed there (except for wild ones like Eleanor Roosevelt) and dads dutifully went off to work for The Company for about forty years.

Men planned for their retirements by learning to tie flies. They stocked up on pastel slacks and white shoes so they could live their golden years in warm climates, slowly spending their comfortable-enough pensions and checking the minutes until sunset on those engraved gold watches The Company had gratefully bestowed upon them.

Today, the guys who must have gold watches buy them for themselves.

And there probably aren't too many men of your generation who will be working for, nor pleasantly retiring from, The Company.

For one thing, The Company probably changed its name and personality in a hostile takeover, leveraged buyout, or megamerger. These days there's not a whole lot of loyalty from either direction. Men and their newer colleagues, working women, skip around from one job to another. It's no longer seen as a detriment to have changed companies. Changing is often the only way to get a better job.

Well, if it's a benefit for those in the workforce, let's see how it can spill over to make life easier for returning mothers. There are, of course, several points of view on the subject, and most are positive.

Helene, who is a judge now, returned to law school when she was thirty. There were many people in her class who were changing careers. One woman was sixty-three, had been a school principal and raised her children, and was now going to try something new.

"Too many women who go back to work take the male ladder point of view, that they have to climb through their careers rung by rung by rung," she says. "But that's not the model for women today, especially mothers who leave work to be home with the children. There are years when you will plateau. Maybe your years at home will be a plateau, an incline, or a decline, but it doesn't matter."

So what happens when you leave the career? It's often wrenching to leave the workforce, but many women continue to struggle to stay in and juggle their responsibilities. Then they feel like failures because there's no happy medium. To be a star in the office, you have to put in more than long hours. It takes a commitment that's tough when you have young children.

Susan is a young mother in her thirties who's thinking about finding her way back to work. She's bright, articulate, and well educated, with a master's degree in business from a prestigious university. A former executive with a major American food company in the Midwest, she now has three children, a successful marriage, a house in the suburbs, and a gnawing ache that something is not right.

Her mom always worked as a teacher. Because of her, Susan wanted to be a high-profile person. She never got on a "girl" track. Her dad was also a teacher and put tremendous academic pressure on her, but she liked working hard. She excelled in math and science and got her undergraduate degree in economics at the University of Michigan. Then she went to business school because it seemed glamorous to her. When she started to work, she thought it was perfect. She helped develop advertising campaigns, did research and marketing that helped the company make important decisions to acquire other companies and pursue new businesses.

"I was so judgmental about moms who stayed home and didn't go back to work," she says. Then her option to go back after a short maternity leave was snatched away when her husband got a new job in another city. She was nine months pregnant with her first child. She couldn't go to the old job and couldn't even work for them part-time. So she was home.

"I felt bad about it. I went against the rules I had set up for myself. I told myself that if I were more energetic, I'd be working. I worried that people thought about me the way I had always thought about mothers who stayed home. I wondered how I'd ever be able to go back to work and face those mothers who had juggled all those years."

Now with her third child, she's become more philosophical, more comfortable with herself.

"I *know* I'll go back to work. I'm bright. I can do things. Since I have a new baby, I imagine I'll be home another five years. Possibly things will change. I have the luxury of a husband with an income that can support the family. I don't have to work, even though that's not what would drive me back."

She had a dream career, she's highly skilled, has loads of connections, but she still doesn't have the vaguest idea how to go back to work.

"How is a company going to look at me?" she asks. "I feel like I don't know how to do anything professional anymore. The whole playing field is different now from when I was working. My son is better on the computer than I am. I can't imagine going back because I can't step in where I was. In fact, I don't even know *where* to step in. I have a real fear of returning. It seems too big to me. Maybe I should just find a charity to volunteer for, to feel good about doing something for me."

Her self-esteem is low. She describes herself like a commodity. She says she needs "retooling, redesigning, new marketing" to reposition herself in the marketplace.

She even wonders whether her daughter in years to come will be ashamed to say, "My mother stayed home with me when I was little."

It's just about impossible to have any perspective on this stage of your life if you begin to question your own worth. Even though it may look insurmountable now, when you're ready to return to a real career, this gap on the resume won't destroy your work life. And you'll know, years from now, that your daughter or son will not be ashamed of the choices their mother made.

There are so many more women who are not taking the straight and narrow path through the working forest and are forging their own. Businesses are going to have to acknowledge that women are telling the truth when they say that they want to come back to work. They just don't always want to come back to the same job. Perhaps when more men request and are granted paternity leaves, when more men want flexible schedules in order to care for their children, more companies will alter their policies.

Valerie, who returned to the workforce twenty years ago as a personnel manager and listens to the worries of her newly married daughter, says, "Women have an advantage in all of this. Because we're often not taken as seriously as men, we have more freedom. It would not end a woman's career if she wanted to go home for a while, but it would pretty much end a man's. I know a woman who left a very big job in business for two years to be with her babies. When she wanted to come back, her original job wasn't available, but she was sent to another city in a commensurate job. This would never happen to a man."

You don't think all this is new, do you? You don't really expect that this is the first time in history that women have worked, stayed with the kids, worked, stayed home, worked? Of course you don't. Because it would figure that mothers before you have wanted to escape from home and orchestrate lives that play their own tune.

Ida Hoos has been crafting her zigzag career since the Depression, when she graduated with a degree in psychology from Radcliffe. With the state of the economy then, she took a job at a department store in Boston, then switched when, by luck, she was offered an opportunity to rehabilitate tuberculosis patients. Another turn of fate sent her to work running a job-training program for welfare recipients.

"Then," says Ida, "in 1942, I committed professional suicide. I got married."

Her work life ceased for the next fourteen years while her concerns centered on her husband and two daughters. When her children were old enough, she went back for a doctorate in sociology at Harvard and in the midfifties wrote her dissertation on automation, which would become the next focus of her career.

Through the years, she's worked in space sciences, systems analysis, and radioactive-waste disposal; she's written books, taught classes, lectured around the world, and served on a presidential task force. "It happened through synergy and serendipity," she says. All the while she still juggled child-raising and running the house. And today, sixty years after she began working, she still writes an article now and then if she's asked.

"You always think that in order to be successful in your work you have to be like men," she says, "disconnected from your everyday life. But I learned that the only reality of your life as a mother, and the only way to be successful, is to know what time you have to be there to pick up the children."

Ida is in her eighties and still working. How old are you? You could be looking at a long, happy life in your new career. Twenty years? Thirty? Why should time out now make a difference? Stay open to the world around you. Listen, watch, feel out new opportunities. Go back to work. Then go home again. Do what you need to do. Then have the courage to carry it out.

From the other side of the desk, you'll put other moms back to work.

As a mom, the boss of the kids, you have a quite a lot of job-creation power. There are basements to clean, floors to scrub, beds to make, rooms to straighten, lost sneakers to find. You're always ready to put anybody in your house to work.

And you'll probably agree that it's often tough to get them to comply. You've heard complicated excuses, temper tantrums, slamming doors, vintage whines. Nevertheless, you've gotten these people to work for you and maybe even made them feel good about their contributions.

You understand that to do their jobs well they need support and encouragement, from pats on the back to equal pay for equal work.

You know starting out means showing them basics such as actually folding T-shirts, then letting them put their own creative stamp on it.

You realize they need bonuses, vacations, flextime, and a few encouraging words.

Gee, wouldn't you like to work for somebody like yourself?

Chances are, when you go back to work, you might. Today about 12 percent of the workforce is employed by women (many of whom are mothers). Women go into business for themselves one and a half times more than men do today.

Other women in the workforce can be very helpful to you. Women out there have lived every nightmare about work you ever dreamed of. They know that stuff about the Old Boy Network and have made great strides in creating support systems for one another and asking employers for help. At McDonald's, for example, women who operate their own franchises have a strong active network in which they share their experience, ideas, and advice.

But you don't have to wait until you join a corporation to find other women. You won't have to look much further than the bulletin board at your health club. Tucked in among the flyers for sports drinks, basketball leagues, and fencing lessons are notices for meetings of working mothers, returning mothers, mothers in similar businesses. They get together to trade stories, contacts, and baby-sitters.

And when you're ready to talk to women in the workforce, they'll be ready to talk to you. You probably have a friend who can introduce you to someone like Justine. She's back at her career in banking after having been at home with her children. Since she understands what returning mothers are going through, she gladly takes those calls from friends of friends and finds time to sit down with women who need information about changing their lives. She says, "I will sit down with women, give them advice and phone numbers of people to call, but I can't promise to hire them on the spot." Have reasonable expectations when you have the chance to visit somebody in her office. It's a real abuse of the opportunity to come in asking for a job.

Dorie Lenz, who has her own television interview program, is always getting calls from women who want to get into television—or anything. She gives the same advice to all of them. "So many women your age are looking for work that it's tough. You have to have something to sell. Get savvy. Interview everybody you can about a field you like. Be passionate about the work you want to do. Nobody wants to hire somebody who doesn't care."

She sends women to nonprofit organizations, which are always looking for people to work very hard. You can learn a lot there and get a lot of responsibility very quickly. She also encourages women to make an appointment with a career-services agency where they can be tested, then directed into an area in which they can be successful.

"And if you should find that you'd be suited to the television industry, don't think you're going to come in as a middle-aged producer, director, or star," she says. "Try to get into the financial office or the traffic department of a local station. You might be able to maneuver a little in these departments and get promotions." She also suggests that women look into radio. "You can do very nicely selling radio time to advertisers. It's very hospitable to women."

It's one thing to get the job, another thing to keep it. (Do I sound like a mother here?) And the women who help you figure out how to get into the workforce can be very helpful in telling you how to stay there successfully.

First, it's important to understand what holding a job is all about. Justine advises, "You have to be a team player. That means being at work on time, getting your job done, and realizing your commitments to your job and fellow workers. You also have to be organized so that your personal matters can be managed.

"Today there are very few offices that will tolerate a prima donna. They are very easy to spot. They think that because they're older and they're important in their communities, they should get big salaries and big perks without paying their dues. You always hear them talking about their expectations."

If you want to be a good employee, think of what you can give a company, not what you can take from it. Dorie tells returning mothers to understand that in each organization there is a sense of territory everywhere. "Make certain you are no threat to anybody. A newcomer is always suspect. So don't come in thinking you know everything. Be reasonably humble during your initial testing period. Be quiet until the rest of the gang knows who you are."

You'll have a new appreciation for all that working mothers go through when you're back in the workforce. Many of the returning mothers who understand the perils women face have gone to great lengths to make the world safe for working women. And you'll be a beneficiary.

One of these women is Donna Lieberman, an A.C.L.U. attorney in New York. She spent a year at home with her first child before she went back to work and believes that women should take as much time with their children as they need.

"The women I supervise are lucky to have me when they get pregnant," she says. "I place a real premium on the needs of the mother. I had a big fight with one woman in my office because she wanted to come back after just three months. It seemed like ten minutes to me. I wanted her to have the appropriate amount of support. Yes, I had to get her commitment on when she was coming back—and I hate asking questions like that—but I wanted her to take stock of herself."

Donna has seen all kinds of pregnancy issues in her case files. There was a woman deckhand on the Staten Island ferry in New York, who after she got the job became an instant celebrity. But the minute she became pregnant, they replaced her with a man and gave her a desk job. As if she suddenly couldn't handle it.

And the men who worked on the ferry were upset because if she got her old job back, then she'd be taking away the job of the man who had replaced her. (And didn't they think a man's income was more important to the family?) Donna's office helped her get her job back. She had her baby and planned to go back as a deckhand after a decent maternity leave.

Many women call Donna's office when they want to extend maternity leave or negotiate a flexible schedule. "We're known for supporting these women," she says. "I always tell them, 'Take time for yourself. Feel good about going back to work.'"

Other women who have gone back have decided it's not even worth it to deal with working for men and trying to get them to understand what women need. They don't think it's worth it for you either, and they only employ working mothers and returning mothers.

The returning mothers welcome it. Andrea thinks she was very lucky to find the women who run the health-care management company she works for. She came to them in her fifties, after her three children were out of high school, and they hired her as a secretary.

"The women I work for are very understanding," says Andrea, who needed to go to work to have more money for her children's college expenses. "They know many of us have families and all kinds of other commitments. They were home themselves when their children were small. A lot of the women here work part-time, but I needed the extra money and work full-time. This job has been a great training ground for me. I learned a lot and have such confidence. Now I'm going to look for a better secretarial job because I'm ready for more, and I know I can do it."

Caroline and Lorna, two women who head an organization that hires working mothers, both turned aside comfortable-until-old-age niches in big, established law firms to run their lives according to their own rhythms and interests.

Caroline is a graduate of Harvard Law School from a time when few women were grudgingly offered that privilege. She clerked for a wise, perceptive judge after she graduated, then entered an old-line law firm. Lorna had an impressive law-school record, too, clerked for the same judge, and got a job at an equally prestigious firm.

Many years later, after Caroline and Lorna had both discovered that this staid form of existence was not for them, the judge brought them together. He was developing an ethics center for lawyers at a prominent law school and thought they'd be just right to manage the program.

Caroline had hated private practice, with its focus on prestige and where your name goes on the letterhead. Instead, she turned her focus to her children and was always looking for something new to do. At an institute for paralegal training, she dreamed up courses and then helped place these bright and energetic students. When the school asked her to be dean, she didn't want to take on the whole time-consuming task and asked a friend who had some experience whether she wanted to share the job. It was a whole new concept.

At the same time, she was also involved in her community, helped found a school where her kids ended up going, and became very active in running it. It took total energy to live this life, but it's what she wanted to spend her energy on.

When she had become quite content with her life, her husband decided that after eighteen years he was leaving. And since he disappeared as a force in the caretaking of the children, it changed the kind of job she could have. She had to be flexible.

"The judge came to me at the right time," Caroline says. "As we developed the center, I saw that the best people who were willing to work with us in an academic setting were women who had responsibility for their kids or aged parents. Many men coming in as a manager would see this as a deficit. But I knew that anyone who raises kids is responsible. They know how to say no and yes and to be honest. Every skill they use in work, they use in life and vice versa."

Lorna came to the continuing-education group after a teaching stint, too, in a law school. Her understanding of the problems that working mothers face came from her own experience. When she was pregnant with her daughter, she was at a big fancy firm and told the partners that she was interested in coming back to work part-time. Their reaction was less than sympathetic. One woman partner, who had taken only three weeks' maternity leave with each of her children, told Lorna that she would do damage to all working women as a whole if she worked part-time. The reason: She would be proving that women had to have special favors.

Then a male partner told her that she would harm herself and be treated as a second-class citizen in the firm if she worked part-time.

"I was told I wouldn't get the good work and that even if I came back full-time later, no one would respect me. I didn't care what they said. I stayed home five months, then went back three days a week."

Though she'd left the firm and been teaching, when the judge called she was ready to go to work with Caroline.

Many women Lorna and Caroline have hired have part-time schedules because they need flexibility. One always thought she would work full-time, but her second child was diabetic, and so it was easier for her to manage her child's illness if she worked part-time. Another was paid to work twenty hours a week, couldn't always finish her work in the office, so also worked on a computer at home.

"I really believe in the notion of pairing up and sharing a job," Caroline says. "I try to do it with everybody. If someone wants to work three days a week, I say, 'Have you got a friend who can do it with you?' It gives you somebody to talk to about your job. And we're not hierarchical. We make up titles if we need them.

"When the women asked for a phone line they could use so their children could call in, I said, 'Sure, just don't ask me to answer that phone.'"

Caroline and Lorna make it clear to the women in the office that children are always welcome. Caroline brought her children in to help out, too, when they were younger.

"They were good, cheap workers," Caroline says. "I have no right to make a mother feel bad because she has to bring her kid to work sometimes. Running this business is like being a mom and running the house."

They've both seen that women put their mom skills to work when they're in a job. "You can translate the skills very easily," says Lorna. "Once when I taught a continuing-education class to some lawyers, one asked me one ridiculous question after another, trying to show that I didn't know as much about the law as he did. It was so tiresome. Finally, I looked at him and said, 'Will you just sit there and be quiet.' I treated him like a belligerent child. I think that women always have the mother identity in their heads. Concentrating on being a mother keeps you more open to the human aspect of life."

In a mall in suburban Cleveland at lunchtime, mothers and their young children fill the food court. They sit around the whooshing fountains while they nibble hot dogs, tacos, Chinese food, and frozen yogurt. Upstairs, watching them from in front of her shop, is Gail Gordon, who knows that someday these mothers will look outside their homes for fulfillment. And that they'll come upstairs before they go back to work to find the new professional wardrobe they're going to need. Gail owns a store that is filled with the suits, blouses, and accessories that can return many mothers to work.

Gail didn't get a Social Security number until she was forty. In fact, she never planned to go to work. But breast cancer changed all that. It took her eighteen months to finish her chemotherapy, and then she knew she had to do something.

"I didn't know how much time I had left, and I didn't want to think that I had frittered away my life sitting around in the suburbs."

Now she does consultations for returning mothers, advising them on everything from makeup to shoes. She'll go into your home and look at your clothes. If you can't afford everything new, she'll remake the suits you have. "It's important for women to know how to put themselves together," she believes. "When you go to an interview, you don't want them to look at anything but your face. You have to wear the right thing. I even have good-luck hankies, and the women all call and tell me whether they got the job."

But she goes beyond the outside appearance. She works with a psychologist, and together they present seminars in the store to help women going back to work feel good about themselves. These women have so many fears in looking for a job. Some have to go to work. Others have husbands who don't want them to work. Some say if they were men, they'd be making a lot more money and that they wouldn't be called back for a fifth interview. They feel so conflicted. Gail and the psychologist reaffirm the notion that every woman should do something for herself, that they have to be persistent and that nothing comes easy.

She should know.

She got married when she was eighteen and had few expectations beyond living a very comfortable life. She had three children all nicely spaced two years apart and put all her efforts into her children and charity work.

"I used to sit around our pool with my two best friends and play canasta. We'd say, 'We put so much into this volunteer work, we should be paid. We'd be great in business.' So we decided to open a shop where we'd sell fine linens. We got our husbands to bankroll us."

Before they could start it, Gail got breast cancer. That didn't stop her. They opened stores one, two, three—there was one for each of them to run. Gail loved working, especially the buying and merchandising.

It was not to last. Her husband told her that they had to move to Columbus for *his* men's clothing stores.

"I was devastated. My friends decided that without my doing the buying, our business was nothing. We folded it. One woman went back to playing tennis. One got another job in real estate. I was forty-seven and had nothing to do."

But she had an idea of what would make her happy. In Columbus she took three thousand square feet of her husband's store and sold very expensive, trendy women's clothes. "Some of the manufacturers' reps asked me to do something for working women, to make them more fun because they were too serious and trying to dress like men in preppy suits and ties.

"I brought in three hundred suits for women and did unbelievably well. I knew that women were looking for more style at work. They wanted to express themselves, and I helped them do it."

Still, she was desperate to get back to Cleveland, to the life and friends she missed so much. She got back, but it took a divorce to get her there. "When I became successful, my husband was very jealous. He'd been pretty much absent while the children were growing up, but things in the house still revolved around him. He was a needy man who needed me to be needy. That was how I was when I met him. It's not what I became.

"After my husband left me, I had little self-esteem. I still couldn't believe I was successful at what I was doing. I went to a psychiatrist for some help. And now I know that I am a bright, capable woman. When I found that I could do all of this—run my own business, have a great time, and do well at it—I realized that I didn't need him to be happy."

Gail had a date recently who asked her, "Why do you work?"

"Because I enjoy it," she told him.

"I make enough money so that no wife of mine would have to work," he said.

"I looked at him and said, 'Who do you think you are? I don't need you. Take me home.' He did!"

She has a life she loves now. She's accomplished what she wanted to in the stores. She's cornered the market and even started her own collection by knocking off high-priced lines.

"And I work with terrific women," she says. "I only hire women. My part-timers are all working mothers. Sometimes we run into problems. The yet-to-be mothers don't understand why I give the mothers certain days off and why I don't get hysterical if a working mother has to run out unexpectedly. That's what you have to do."

Gail is both mother and psychologist to the women who work for her. They need her help a lot, and they're always there for one another.

"I think it's going to be easier for the girls who are growing up now," she says. "They expect to grow up and go to work. My granddaughter does. Ask her what she wants to be, and she says, 'a doctor or a lawyer.' She sees it as a matter of pride.

She says she feels like she's on her sixth life: kid, married woman, mother, businesswoman, divorced woman, grandma. But her granddaughter sees Gail one way. She says, "I love my grandma because she owns a store, she lets me work, and she pays me."

There will come a day when the judge's robe, surgeon's mask, Armani suit, corner office, membership in an airline club, and key to the executive washroom are all within your grasp.

Yours.

Not your husband's, your father's, your mother's, your supposedly brilliant neighbor's.

It will be *your* airline-club membership that admits you into that comfortable oasis in the middle of a tumultuous airport. The invitation to the White House will come because of *your* work. And that new job offer complete with six figures, stock options, and a new car in the garage will be made to you.

You're smirking because you know you'll be going into that new job at the ripe old age of, well, let's say over thirty-five. You've used up your twenties already. How are you going to reap the benefits that women who went to work and stayed there are savoring already?

Keep in mind you're not the first mom to go back to work.

Or the first one to have high ambitions for yourself.

Didn't Patty Murray run for the United States Senate as the mom in tennis shoes? She won! Our ambassador to the United Nations, Madeleine Albright, was at home in the suburbs of New York raising her three daughters for years before she ever went to work.

As a matter of fact, Albright listened at her 1959 Wellesley graduation to a speaker who told the class that their job was to raise the next generation. But Albright, the daughter of a Czechoslovakian diplomat, went on to work toward graduate degrees in political science from Columbia University. All the while she was home with the children, playing tennis and giving parties for her husband's colleagues, too.

It wasn't until she moved to Washington (for her husband's

career) that she pursued a career of her own. She started out innocently—as a volunteer fund-raiser for presidential candidate Edmund Muskie in the early seventies. But her credentials, talent, and intelligence earned her a new position when Muskie later appointed her his chief legislative assistant. From there, she was on a roll—as a congressional liaison for the National Security Council, a professor at Georgetown, policy adviser to presidential candidates, and now an ambassador.

Like her father. But this career is hers.

How do you know when you've suddenly made it, when you're transformed from a mom to a worker to a real leader? Sometimes others will see it before you do. You feel as though you're traveling in disguise, that you're not really that woman in the corner office. You're really an impostor who only *seems* as though she can do a competent job. That's your secret, and you wonder when they'll figure it out—and pray that they don't.

When you know what you want out of your career, you know where you want to be and you work hard to get it, you might be *amazed*, but you'll be very sure you've reached it. And those fleeting glimpses of your other self will become more and more like a dream.

Norita, the stockbroker, knew that she had done well in her business when she began to receive requests to speak to women's groups about investments and finance. She was regarded as an expert. She talks to women business owners about managing their assets. And she speaks to groups of women about empowerment in the workplace.

"I didn't realize I could be so successful at this," says Norita.

"But I know why. It was my love of my work that got me here. I wanted to deal with women who need financial advice, and they saw I was honest and on their side."

In her business everybody—men and women—gets the same commission. It's a set fee. But she worked hard, and it paid off. She's won awards from her company and has been honored at recognition dinners.

"It's funny," she says, "I never could have done this when my children were young. There would have been too many intrusions. I am at work at eight. I could not have devoted the same kind of time when I had little children."

Ann Gaither, who runs her family's tire-distribution business, is not surprised by her success. Taking over the business was not difficult for her. She knew what her company's message was and could deliver that message over and over because she believed in it strongly.

"Often I had to prove myself, but that was okay. I knew that I wanted to be successful. I don't know how to do anything halfway, although when I came in here I didn't understand the role I was going to play one day."

It really helps if a woman has a path, she says. "You either walk into a company and say, 'Well, this is how it is, and I'm going to fit into the structure.' Or you scan the room and say, 'When I'm president, things are going to be different.' Know where you're going. Then you'll never be tripped up, and you can become quite focused."

This doesn't mean the mothers without a plan will be any less successful. It does means their personalities can accommodate more spontaneity. They'll find they are *quite* surprised at what they can do and where they can go. Even more, by where they end up.

Nancy, a highly respected banker, went to work not knowing the first steps to take, not even what kind of job she could do. Her success came early, her plan later.

She went to college, married, and graduated quite pregnant. After staying home for a year, she went to graduate school in history. She had two more children. Eventually, she wanted to work but didn't want to teach history and had no idea how you got a job if you didn't want to be a secretary or teacher.

She was living in New York in the sixties, and someone told her to try working for city government in Mayor Lindsay's administration. She got a job in child welfare as assistant to a bureau director, was promoted to principal assistant, and finally took over as bureau director. "You can rise in government," she says, "but the inadequate compensation doesn't attract the great-est people. Just when I realized I didn't like city government as a career, I was recruited by a foundation to be the director."

The foundation centered its interests in crime and justice and problems of aging, and Nancy was in charge of giving out money. "It was wonderful to be able to be generous," she says. Still, she didn't see this as a career. Four years later, she started to look again.

This time she approached it methodically, planning to get it right. She set up criteria for both the company and industry she wanted to go into. She wanted a big company, one that she could stay with, one that provided a wide possibility for lateral moves. She wanted to work, but she didn't want to be doing the same exact job forever, so she had to go to a place where there were different departments.

She looked at insurance and investment banking, which weren't right. Then she looked at banks. Many of them met her criteria, but when she talked to people there, they didn't really know what to do with her. One bank had a job available in public affairs, but that's not what she wanted.

Then luck came into it. She shared a cab with a man who said he would make a call for her to be seen by someone he knew at another bank. She made an appointment, and at the meeting she knew this was the company where she wanted to be. Even though she came in through a contact, she was hired on her own abilities. You want somebody to see you as a favor but not to hire you as a favor.

When she accepted the job, she took a significant step back in terms of compensation. "But I spoke to my employers honestly about where I wanted to go in the bank," says Nancy. "Even though I had never worked in banking, I was offering them my talents plus a lot of life experiences. I needed them to look at me with an open mind. They told me that I would move accordingly."

Most employers try and speak to you truthfully and then try to do what they say. They can't afford to hire you just to be nice. If they promise you something, and you hold up your side of the bargain, you'll probably get the better jobs, bonuses, and responsibilities. That's what happened with Nancy. After six months, she had a review. Both sides had done what they'd promised, and she had a salary increase.

"Now I'm in a position to hire women who are looking for ways to get back into the workforce," says Nancy. "I understand those life experiences and how they contribute to who you are and what you can do for an organization."

Once you get where you're going, many doors open for you. Take the boardroom, for instance. Twenty years ago many corporate boards saw the light and started finding women directors—but only because they were women. Today, boards still seek women because they're women, but also because of their professional expertise.

One good way that's been recommended for women to get into the board network is to go onto the board of a nonprofit organization. They're always looking for basic help. From there, take a look at the workings of your local government, school, or religious organization.

Getting involved in professional organizations of your chosen field also makes you known to your colleagues, which is another sign that you're a leader. It also builds your confidence to take a stand on how your industry is regarded. In my field of advertising, there are lots of groups and clubs and organizations to join, all with committees that need volunteers, boards that need members, and offices that need elected officials. And if you're just coming into your new career, it helps to network.

When you go back to work, there's no need to contain your ambition. In fact, this is the time to realize that you deserve all

you can achieve. It really depends on your attitude, your willing-
ness to open your eyes to the world around you and to experience as much of it as possible. Success doesn't happen only to
those with the most connections, the biggest bank accounts, and
largest reserves of self-confidence. But it is more likely that success comes to those who are most willing to forgo ideas of what
life is *supposed* to be like and what they're *supposed* to do. And it
often helps to have a role model, a woman who has achieved and
who gives you some guidance.

Barbara Woodhouse never had any idea that she would go
from being a suburban housewife/mother to being a law-school
professor. These days, her former boss, Supreme Court Justice
Sandra Day O'Connor, refers to Barbara when she talks about
giving chances to women who want to be lawyers.

Barbara, who teaches family law at the University of
Pennsylvania School of Law, did not go to college right after
high school. She traveled, then married a very traditional man
when she was twenty-two, got pregnant right away, and stayed
home while he went to work. By the time they had a second
child, she was getting ready for her next life by taking college
courses one at a time. She and her husband talked about her
going to work when the kids were in school, "but my real job
was being with them. I did all the mom things. I was on the
board of the nursery school, I was a Brownie leader. Everything
I did was built around family and children."

Still, she was thinking about what she could do. "I wanted
work that gave me some kind of status. I was sick of being in
community meetings and saying things that no one paid any
attention to, but when some lawyer said the exact same thing,

people thought it was brilliant. I knew I was as smart as they were, I just didn't have a college degree."

Since she really couldn't go to college full-time, she got into a program in New York State that allowed her to do course work on her own, then take proficiency exams, and finally earn a degree.

After getting the degree, what she really wanted was to be trained to do something. She thought she'd start as an entry person in computers or marketing. Then she thought she'd go for specialized training like a paralegal. Then it occurred to her that she could be a lawyer.

She applied to law school and got into Pace, a small school in New York City, but she had really wanted to go to Columbia University Law School. She knew that it would be tough to get into a highly competitive school like Columbia and that the admissions office wouldn't understand her rather unusual undergraduate experience. She wanted to talk to the admissions people herself, but you don't have interviews for law school the way you do for undergraduate admissions. One day she borrowed her best friend's wine-colored blazer, went down to Columbia, and talked her way in.

"I was wavering because the money was difficult. When I was trying to decide between Pace and Columbia, one family friend said, 'For what Barbara wants to do, Pace is enough.' How did he know what I wanted to do? Why were there modest expectations?"

Women admitted to Columbia are invited to Myra Bradwell Day at the law school, which is a special event sponsored by the Women's Law Group. Barbara went to a panel of prominent women lawyers chaired by Professor Ruth Bader Ginsburg. It was a watershed for her.

"The hardest thing had always been to imagine myself as a lawyer. My vision of a lawyer was not a woman, certainly not me. There were no women lawyers in my town back in 1980 when I was applying to law school. But right in front of me were intelligent, funny, marvelous women talking about their lives. They weren't so different from me. In fact, they were just like my friends."

She enrolled at Columbia, and when she was getting ready to graduate, she had to think about what she would do the next year. Many of her classmates were applying for clerkships with state and federal judges, even Supreme Court justices. She wondered whether to go for a Supreme Court clerkship but let it slide.

Her husband asked, "What about those applications? Did you apply to the Supreme Court yet?"

"How could I leave you and the kids for a year?" she asked.

"That's ridiculous," he replied. "Go ahead."

When you apply for a Supreme Court clerkship, you don't apply to a particular justice. You're told where to go, and Barbara got a clerkship with Justice O'Connor.

"I breathed a sigh of relief to see that other clerks on the Court were married with children. Justice O'Connor was quite interested in my path. She told me that she worked when her children were quite small and then stayed at home with them for several years before practicing law again. When my family came to town to visit, she wouldn't let me work. She'd say, 'Your family is too important.'"

Barbara's son Kenny used to make model airplanes for Justice O'Connor, who would display them on a shelf in her office. O'Connor once called him on his birthday and told him that when she was a little girl she had gone to school in the city, away from her parents. She told him she had missed her family and thanked Kenny for lending her his mother.

"It's an example of the way she recognized I didn't have to pretend I didn't have a family," says Barbara.

Once she mentioned that her daughter was in an operetta at school.

"You're going, of course," said O'Connor.

"I can't," she answered.

"This is a must-attend event," O'Connor replied as she dialed the number of her travel agent.

As a law professor today, Barbara has chaired umpteen panels for women who worry about their careers and families.

"I remember as a mother feeling defensive and undervalued. I needed to get out of the house, to have some intellectual stimulation and a break. I was lucky to get that break."

So when she learned that Justice O'Connor was coming to Philadelphia to honor a woman judge, Barbara wrote her former boss a letter telling her how much her example and that of Justice Ginsburg had meant in giving her confidence to do more than she ever thought she could.

They spent time together that day, and a couple of young women lawyers came up to the hotel to meet O'Connor. "They were very nervous being with the Justice. She was wearing a scarf, and I complimented her on it. She turned to these two young women and started telling them ways you could use a scarf as a fashion accessory. They looked amazed that she was talking to them one woman to another. That was a little gift she gave them, and I'm sure they'll never forget it, especially when they wear a scarf the way a Supreme Court justice told them to do it."

Later that day when she gave out the award Justice O'Connor said, "We know the power of simply seeing a woman actually doing a job. It gives people who are forming their own identity at whatever age a strength that gets passed back and forth over the years."

You can be proud of your children's accomplishments and your own all at the same time.

I'm still in the middle of all of this.

My children are little enough—a second-grader and a fourth-grader—that I know I still want to be within shouting distance when they need me.

And I'm big enough to know that if I don't work, I'll never be able to afford computers and colleges, I'll get boring, and I'll wake up in eleven years bereft and miserable because my only interests in life have gone off to college.

But I'm also lucky. I learned very early that I was not one of those moms who could have it all, all at the same time. I can't even read while the television is on in the next room.

So I've learned to take my life in little pieces. That's what the mothers in this book have done, too. Each of them has said they never could have been as successful at work had they returned full-time when their children were small. I know that feeling. It's very difficult to give your all to a project when you aren't sure whether you can get a baby-sitter at the last minute so that you can stay late at the office.

Having kids is really distracting from your work, too. That's why I had to work freelance. Even then I would sit in meetings and think, "I'll bet I'm the only person in this room who has diapers, wipies, and a pacifier in her purse."

When you're home you do get a wonderful satisfaction: when your children sing the songs, say the rhymes, or do the lit-tle dances you taught them or exhibit some kind of exemplary behavior such as sharing their toys when you didn't even ask them to. It shows you that you can do something. And imagine, you don't even get any training for this. At least when you go back to work you can choose an area in which you have some expertise.

But you know what? You've given your children that good start, sent them off to live a life in which you imagine you've given them enough warnings, guidance, and encouragement to make the right choices.

You've taught them that life is not about being rich, winning every single competition, always being first in line, getting to sit in the front seat, or standing up and shouting to make sure everyone hears your opinion.

You've passed along the notion that good people like them-selves, have principles, and accept responsibility.

It's time to put those kids in another part of your brain.

Stop thinking about them every second.

This time it's about you. Returning to work means you have to decide who you want to be besides Mommy.

Go in and discover that woman in there who's got the talent to put more into life. The stories you've read have shown you that mothers exactly like you—who got married very young or didn't finish college or thought they were incapable of landing any sort of job—can do it!

And the rewards are extraordinary.

You have money of your own. You have a renewed vitality, an increased interest in the world around you. And you know so much more. Whole new worlds you never concerned yourself with are open to you. You're interested in new people, and new people are interested in you.

You have something to do that makes you feel very good about yourself.

And even your children can have a whole new respect for you.

One mother who stayed home for years before going to work told me that when her daughter had her first child she said, "Mom, I'm not going back to work for at least three years. I want to do it just the way you did."

So you see, you'll still be a good mother.

And you'll be an even better woman.

OUACHITA TECHNICAL COLLEGE
LIBRARY/LRC

3 9005 00003 1611